"What an exceptional book! First, its scope is different from other books in that it focuses exclusively on the Psalms—all 150 of them. Second, its format is unique because the author presents each divinely inspired song with creative divisions such as 'Musical Notes' (how the psalm reveals God and his grace) and 'Sing the Song' (suggestions for personal application). If you're a woman looking for a fresh approach to your study of Scripture, you'll find it in Lydia Brownback's *Sing a New Song*."

> **Donald S. Whitney,** professor of biblical spirituality and associate dean, School of Theology, The Southern Baptist Theological Seminary; author, *Spiritual Disciplines for the Christian Life* and *Praying the Bible*

"I'm grateful for this call to read the book of Psalms straight through! Lydia Brownback has distilled the various themes and offers great encouragement for readers to delve into the prayers and praises of God's people given in his Word. How good to be reminded that the psalms speak into all the moments of our lives, giving us a song for each one."

> **Kathleen B. Nielson,** author; speaker; senior adviser, The Gospel Coalition

"Not only do we need to embrace our emotional side as humans, but as Christians we want to learn a vocabulary that can make our feelings for God be contagious to others. Enter the Psalms. God not only gave us a whole book of Scripture for learning the language of the heart, he also made it the longest book of all. Join me in making it a daily habit to open your Bible first to the Psalms each morning, and let Lydia Brownback help your reading and meditation stay true and go deep. *Sing a New Song* is a valuable companion for a lifelong journey through the ups and downs, joys and griefs, praises and laments of God's own inspired book for the Christian's heart."

> **David Mathis,** executive editor, desiringGod.org; pastor, Cities Church, Minneapolis; author, *Habits of Grace: Enjoying Jesus through the Spiritual Disciplines*

"Lydia Brownback brings 'the heart of the Old Testament'—the Psalms—to the hearts of her readers. If you desire to deepen your walk with the triune God of the Psalter, Brownback's brilliant book will shed light on the brilliance of our Lord's providential purposes for his people. It will inspire you to read and reread the Psalms. To use them devotionally. Pray them. Sing them! See them as a mirror to your soul and a reflection of the greatness of our God."

Douglas Sean O'Donnell, senior pastor, Westminster Presbyterian Church, Elgin, Illinois; author, *The Beginning and End of Wisdom*; editor, *The Pastor's Book*

"Sisters in Christ, come journey through the book of Psalms and gaze afresh at our God of steadfast love and covenantal faithfulness. Lydia Brownback has given us an instructive, strengthening gift for heart and mind. Study the biblical text; discover the fulfillment of promises in the New Testament; bring your praise, laments, joys, and fears; pour out your heart, trusting his care and grace for us."

Jane Patete, former coordinator of women's ministry, the Presbyterian Church in America

Sing a New Song

Other Crossway Books by Lydia Brownback

Contentment: A Godly Woman's Adornment

Finding God in My Loneliness

Joy: A Godly Woman's Adornment

Purity: A Godly Woman's Adornment

Trust: A Godly Woman's Adornment

A Woman's Wisdom: How the Book of Proverbs Speaks to Everything

Sing a New Song

A Woman's Guide to the Psalms

LYDIA BROWNBACK

WHEATON, ILLINOIS

Library of Congress Cataloging-in-Publication Data
Names: Brownback, Lydia, 1963– author.
Title: Sing a new song : a woman's guide to the Psalms / Lydia Brownback.
Description: Wheaton, Illinois : Crossway, [2017] | Includes bibliographical references.
Identifiers: LCCN 2017005593 (print) | LCCN 2017032954 (ebook) | ISBN 9781433554346 (pdf) | ISBN 9781433554353 (mobi) | ISBN 9781433554360 (epub) | ISBN 9781433554339 (trade paperback) | ISBN 9781433554360 (ePub) | ISBN 9781433554353 (Mobipocket)
Subjects: LCSH: Bible. Psalms—Devotional literature.
Classification: LCC BS1430.54 (ebook) | LCC BS1430.54 .B76 2017 (print) | DDC 223/.207082–dc23
LC record available at https://lccn.loc.gov/2017005593

With gratitude to the Good Shepherd
for leading me to green pastures, still waters,
and paths of righteousness
through faithful men:

Todd Augustine
Kevin Bervik
James Montgomery Boice
Jerry Bridges
Marion Clark
Geoff Dennis
Bill Edgar
Sinclair Ferguson
Allan Fisher
Richard Gaffin
Mark Goodrich
Jonathan Inman
Jeff Mills
J. I. Packer
Richard Phillips
Leland Ryken
Philip Ryken

Contents

THE PSALTER, BOOK 2

THE PSALTER, BOOK 3

THE PSALTER, BOOK 4

THE PSALTER, BOOK 5

Preface

Sing a new song! The call is sprinkled throughout the psalms to express the joy of new blessings received from God's hand. Those blessings weren't limited to the psalmists' days; they are meant for us as well. That's one reason Psalms is the most universally loved book of the Bible. Its appeal isn't so much the poetry or the musical aspects but what it conveys about God himself—that he welcomes the honest outpouring of his people's hearts. Joy, sorrow, anger, fear, perplexity, discouragement, and longing—the entire spectrum of human emotions—are reflected in the psalms and taken to God in prayerful song. And each psalm reveals particular facets of God himself.

Sing a New Song is a springboard, a launching-off place, for going deeper into the psalms in all kinds of ways. Here are a few suggestions:

- *Build confidence in prayer.* The heartfelt prayers of the psalmists build our confidence to approach God with our personal pleas and pains. They also guide the substance of our prayers. We don't know God's will in all its particulars, but we can be sure that the prayer requests of the psalmists are God's will because they are part of Scripture, and we can adapt them to our own situations. How did the psalmists pray in a crisis, and what did they ask for? How did they approach God after a fall into sin? How did praying give them perspective in difficult relationships? Scan each entry in *Sing a New Song* for prayer aids.

- *Prepare a Bible study.* Gather a group of women to study the psalms (see appendix 1 for group study suggestions), and use *Sing a New Song* to help you prepare for discussions. In all our Bible studying, we want to be faithful to the biblical text, which requires examining the original context. We want to know the *who, what, where, when, why,* and *how* of the psalmists before we apply what we read to our own

15

circumstances. Looking at the original context provides us with an accurate view of God, which is necessary for real spiritual growth.

- *Journal your emotions.* Let's face it—we women are emotional creatures. And we don't have to apologize for that fact. After all, God designed us this way, and from the psalms we see that God works in and through our emotions to draw us closer to him and to mature us spiritually. As you read each entry in *Sing a New Song*, track the dominant emotions in the psalm. Do they fluctuate from beginning to end, and if so, why? Where is God in the midst of depression? How is anger expressed and dealt with? What causes joy and happiness? If you'd like to get a better handle on your own emotions, consider journaling your way through the psalms. Appendix 2 provides you with an idea for creating such a journal.

- *Weave Psalms with hospitality.* As you will see, the psalms were sung primarily in gatherings of God's people. *Sing a New Song* provides clues about how each psalm was used, and some of what we see can be adapted for use with your own friends and family. During a celebratory season, host a gathering at which each participant reads aloud a portion of a thanksgiving psalm. Or when believers you know suffer rejection or persecution for their faith, gather together to pray one of King David's laments. There are so many possibilities here!

Those are just a few ideas. However you use *Sing a New Song*, the primary aim is to deepen your faith by glimpsing how the psalms shed light on the multifaceted character of our great God and his overarching purposes for his people.

For each psalm you'll find the following sections:

- *Theme.* A one-sentence overview of the psalm.
- *Harmony.* Something about the nature of the psalm and how it fits into the big picture of the Psalter.
- *Singing in Tune.* A verse-by-verse breakdown of the psalm.

- *Musical Notes.* How the psalm reveals God and his grace.
- *Sing the Song.* A suggestion for related Scripture reading and personal application.

On a personal note, this is the most challenging book project I've undertaken to date. The discipline of drawing out the relational nature of the psalms while being faithful to their original context—and doing so 150 unique times—has shown me what a long way I still have to go in my understanding of God and his Word. Challenging as the process has been, the spiritual rewards have been enormous—and surprising. It is my prayer that *Sing a New Song* will profit you in the same way.

The

PSALTER

Book 1

Psalm

❧ 1 ☙

A Blessed Life

THEME

Pursuing God's path leads to flourishing, but following the way of the wicked leads only to destruction.

HARMONY

Psalm 1 has lots of similarity to the teaching and wording of the Bible's Wisdom Literature, primarily the book of Proverbs. The psalms that mirror the wisdom teaching found in Scripture are called "wisdom psalms."

SINGING IN TUNE

Blessed. The very first word of the very first psalm reveals what God wants for his people—blessing. Nothing compares to the reward of living out a close walk with him. Such a walk entails a continual rejection of one way and a wholehearted embracing of another. Truly blessed people are those who guard their hearts from the allure of the world (v. 1) and fixate on the ways of God (v. 2). Turning from worldliness isn't a one-time choice; it's constant—every moment of every day. Whose counsel will guide us? What will fill our time, and with whom will we fill it? The psalmist makes it seem so simple, and it actually *is* that simple—it's just not easy. But by fixating on God's Word, it gets easier. That's because we're changed in the process. Over time, the pull of worldly power is weakened, and our delight in God's ways grows stronger (v. 2). So does our wisdom, for we realize that delighting in God's ways isn't something to do as a way to get more blessing—the delight *is* the blessing. Even so, as we drink in the water of God's Word and ways, we become like a well-watered, fruit-producing tree, and we find that every part of our lives and work and relationships prospers in practical, tangible ways (v. 3). To know this blessing for ourselves, it helps to see the world as it really is. The promises of easy pleasure and avoidance of pain inevitably evaporate into nothing (v. 4), and those who choose that path, rejecting God and those who love him, will be gone (v. 5). In the meantime, the Lord intimately "knows" his own, which means we aren't left to ourselves as we seek to walk with him (v. 6).

MUSICAL NOTES

God's Grace

It's a struggle at times to fixate on God's Word and avoid falling into worldly temptation. There is only one person who ever did—Jesus. He is the only One who has ever lived out Psalm 1 as God intends. But in union with him, we can become the flourishing tree we find in this psalm, because in him are the streams of water that well up to eternal life (John 4:14).

God's Attributes

- all-knowing
- nurturing
- righteous
- wise

SING THE SONG

Read Proverbs 1–2. What similarities to Psalm 1 do you find in those chapters?

way of the Lord
strength in Christ

fear God, cling to Him for direction! Pr. 1:10 – do not let sin entice you
vs 29-31 → knowledge + fear of the LORD
Pr. 2 – value of wisdom WOW!

Help us to seek Law! Die to self
Everyday/each moment

21

2019

Psalm

~~ 2 ~~

Kiss the King

THEME

The king of God's choosing is celebrated because he is a channel of blessing for God's people.

HARMONY

God appointed a line of kings, beginning with David, to lead God's people in his ways. And God promised that through this kingly line would come his greatest blessings (see 2 Sam. 7:12–17). Sure enough, when the kings served faithfully, all the people were blessed. But ultimately they were all failures in faithfulness—every last one—and all God's people suffered for it. Even so, some of the psalms, like Psalm 2, are songs of rejoicing about the king, which can mean only one thing—despite the royal failures, there was still hope. Humans—even kings—fail, but God does not. He always keeps his promises. The ideal King was still to come. Psalms that rejoice in the king are called "royal psalms."

SINGING IN TUNE

Psalm 2 was written in a time much like ours—morally corrupt and politically unstable—yet a note of confidence runs all through it. Threats loom and evil leaders rise, but no plot or plan devised against God and God's people will ultimately succeed (vv. 1–3). In every age, the desire to "cast away" God's authority is lodged in the hearts of some who abuse their power, and underneath their politically correct lingo, they harbor a special hatred for God's people. There is no need for fear, however, because God can break any power in an instant. Evil authorities may strut around with delusions of control, but God isn't wringing his hands with worry about how to uphold his honor. In fact, he laughs at their attempts to be rid of him (v. 4). Lasting security comes not from a strong economy or military might or even from a morally upright society. It comes from taking refuge in God's anointed King, the Son (v. 12). We need not fear who sits on any earthly throne, because Jesus sits enthroned in heaven.

MUSICAL NOTES

God's Grace

Even good leaders fail to live up to their promises, so we cannot rely on them to keep us safe. This was true in the psalmist's day, when even King David (the man anointed by God to lead his people) broke God's law and violated the people's trust. And so did all the kings who came after him. From ancient days up to the present, it's clear that broken human beings are incapable of providing all we hope for in a leader. Only a divine ruler can provide the safety and security we so desperately need and conquer every evil power that threatens (vv. 7–9). King Jesus is that ruler. He is everything that Israelite kings failed to be and that our modern leaders pretend to be. King Jesus will never fail, and his rule will never end. Every other governing authority is temporary, and they possess wisdom to govern only to the degree that they bow before the ultimate authority of King Jesus (vv. 10–12).

God's Attributes

- authoritative
- holy
- powerful
- protecting

SING THE SONG

Describe how Acts 4:24–28; 13:32–39; Hebrews 1:5–8; and Revelation 19:15–16 reveal Jesus as the fulfillment of Psalm 2 and the underlying reason for the victorious confidence so evident among those who sang it.

23

Psalm

3

Nothing to Fear

THEME

God helps and strengthens his people when they are troubled.

HARMONY

Psalm 3 is a lament composed by David.[1] Laments express perplexity, anguish, and even discouragement during times of overwhelming circumstances. Yet they also reflect the confident hope of those who trust their compassionate and faithful God. The psalms of lament teach us that God welcomes boldness and honesty when we cry out to him, and we need not fear that he won't hear, because he has promised never to turn away from those who truly seek him. The particular crisis in view here is recounted in 2 Samuel 15–16.

SINGING IN TUNE

Hated and hunted—that was the plight of King David, and he was at a loss as to how to cope with it. Worst of all, it was his own son who sought to harm him. So real was the threat to his life that David had to flee his home and hide (v. 1). His enemies seemed greater and more numerous than his friends—and what about God? He heard the taunts: "There is no salvation for him in God" (v. 2). But the taunts weren't true. God *was* his protector. God had promised to be faithful no matter what, and his promise included not only protection but also restoration (vv. 3–4). Most of us have never been in David's shoes—hated and hunted by a family member—but no doubt we've been on the receiving end of anger, whether justified or not. At such times, nothing we say or do works to calm the situation and restore reason, and we feel utterly helpless. But we don't have to wait to get to that point to do what David did. He cried aloud to God (v. 4). He poured out his heart, and because God had faithfully answered him in the past, David knew God wouldn't leave him without help in the present (v. 5).

MUSICAL NOTES

God's Grace

After pouring out his heart, so confident was David of God's involvement in his trouble that he was able to get a good night's sleep (v. 5). That's what casting our cares on God really looks like. When evening anxieties are raging, do we hand them over to our heavenly Father? If so—if we have really entrusted our cares to God—we won't lie awake all night with worry. Real trust banishes fear (v. 6), and it inspires even bolder prayer (vv. 7–8).

God's Attributes

- listening
- protecting
- saving
- sustaining

FEAR

SING THE SONG

Do not let your heart be troubled

Explain how John 14:1, 27 and Romans 8:14–17 can help you sing Psalm 3.

children of GOD

Psalm

⤙ 4 ⤚

A Cry for Help

THEME

Those who trust God during difficult seasons are able to wait for his deliverance.

HARMONY

Psalm 4 is a lament, but it is also characterized by restful confidence. This type of psalm reflects the hope of those who trust their compassionate and faithful God. Fear is overruled by faith in the One who has promised never to turn away from his people. Here in Psalm 4, David shows confidence by leaning on the Lord at the end of the day. In this evening prayer he models the security of those who trust.

SINGING IN TUNE

In the midst of difficulty, David cries for God's help, and he remembers how God has relieved him from past distress (v. 1). It seems evident that his distress was prolonged, as ours sometimes is. "How long?" he asks. How long will he have to bear with people who challenge his commitment to the Lord? Despite these pressures, he knows he's safe, because the Lord has claimed him as his own and hears all his prayers (vv. 2–3). David's confidence in God enables him to encourage others to persevere and to resist the desire to retaliate. It's right to be angry when evil gets a foothold, but all too easily, our anger against sin turns *into* sin because we take it personally. Keeping anger in a righteous place requires humility (v. 4). It also requires a trusting heart and a surrendered life (v. 5). Temptation to doubt God's care assails God's people, but they can escape the temptation by asking God for a fresh glimpse of his goodness (v. 6). David well understood what stress is all about. Yet because his confidence rested in God rather than in people or his self-made solutions, he was able to live in peace both day and night (v. 7). We are never more out of control than when we attempt to be *in* control. If a man like David, a king with vast responsibilities, could simply go to bed and fall asleep, then so can we, if we but trust in the Lord.

MUSICAL NOTES

God's Grace

Secure children talk to their parents. They say what they think and express what they feel. And when they want something, they just ask. They don't stop to ponder how to package their words or manage impressions. One reason is that they lack the sophistication to communicate any other way; more importantly, they trust. Whatever they ask and whatever the answer, they know they are loved and cared for. God welcomes the same candor from all those he has set apart for himself in Christ.

God's Attributes

- comforting
- joy-giving
- listening
- trustworthy

SING THE SONG

Sanctify is another word in the Bible for "set apart" (v. 3). From 1 Corinthians 1:2; 6:9–11; Ephesians 5:25–27; and 1 Thessalonians 5:16–24, explain how God sets apart his people.

Psalm

❧ 5 ☙

A Morning Prayer

THEME

Focusing on God changes our perspective on our troubles.

HARMONY

As the king of Israel, David was called to lead God's people in God's ways and to model a godly life of faith. Here in Psalm 5, he leads them in a prayer for the destruction of wicked people. This was no personal vendetta on David's part; he desired the triumph of righteousness over evil. For that reason, psalms that include prayers for destruction are called "imprecatory psalms." In praying this way, David is upholding God's just and holy character. And since the psalm was sung in public, the evildoers might hear of it, be warned, and turn to God themselves.

SINGING IN TUNE

The morning routine. Getting up and ready for the day ahead consumes an hour or two, even when all the details come together like clockwork. It's likely, however, that King David had more on his plate than the busiest among us. We have meetings to lead and homework to check, shirts to iron and lunches to pack, but David had a nation to run. Yet his morning routine included the Lord—not a pass through the verse of the day and a prayer for the hours ahead but an orienting of himself and his life and his troubles upward to God (vv. 1–3). Spending time in God's presence shaped his thoughts and prepared him to view the day ahead from God's perspective. In keeping, as we listen to God in his Word, we are freshly sensitized to the evil of sin (v. 4) and reminded that God's righteousness will prevail in the long run (vv. 5–6). The majority of our waking hours are spent out in the world, not in a quiet room with an open Bible, which is another reason why morning time with the Lord is a precious gift, not a burdensome obligation. Through it we are gifted with the discernment we need to distinguish between truth and error, good and evil, and to pray that God will not allow evildoers to succeed in their sin (vv. 9–10). The Lord, our righteous guide and merciful protector, is always waiting to meet us in the morning.

MUSICAL NOTES

God's Grace

God is so holy that evil cannot dwell with him (v. 4). Because that's true, only his grace enables us to pray with confidence. David knew this, so he took refuge in that grace (v. 11), as we must. As we do, God covers us (v. 12) with the shield provided by Jesus's payment for our sins on the cross. Even the worst evildoer will be spared from God's righteous wrath if she turns to Jesus in faith.

God's Attributes

- just
- merciful
- righteous

Daily focus on Christ. The work HE did on earth for my good and His glory.

SING THE SONG

Read Jesus's parable of the ten virgins (Matt. 25:1–13) and his teaching that follows in Matthew 25:31–46. Where do you find both warning and hope in his words, and where in the teaching is God's mercy revealed?

• be ready
2019 – Let each day be lived for Christ's glory. Help us to know you & love you. Be w/ Christ. family. Barry, & children. Be w/ her sisters & parents.

29

Psalm

※ 6 ※

In Need of Mercy

THEME

God works through painful circumstances to deepen the faith of his people.

HARMONY

Lament psalms sometimes include an acknowledgment of sin. Such is the case in Psalm 6. These songs of repentance, sometimes called "penitential psalms," were prayerfully sung by individuals, as is the case with David here, and other times by God's people as a whole. In either case, we find no anxious fear in these songs, because God is merciful and kind, and he responds to his people's confessions with love and deliverance.

SINGING IN TUNE

If only I hadn't . . . It's the taunt of regret that nags us when the conse- quences of sin come home to roost. The suffering we bring on ourselves is uniquely bitter, as David knew firsthand. Although we don't know specifically that a particular sin was the source of his suffering in this psalm, it is clearly a possibility. Either way, a choice for sin is a choice for weariness, sorrow, the breaking of good relationships, and entrapment in bad ones (vv. 6–7). Worst of all, sin mars our enjoyment of God and can lead to painful discipline (vv. 1–3). Even so, in the very midst of our sin-induced pain, we can cry out to God for deliverance (vv. 2, 4–5) and expect it with confidence and hope—not because we determine to get our spiritual act together or because we've found a way to justify what we've done but because God is loving and kind (v. 4). Deliverance begins before we've even finished praying for it, as it did for David (vv. 8–9), with a renewed awareness that God is for us, and because of that, everything aligned against us, including our besetting temptations, cannot defeat us.

MUSICAL NOTES

God's Grace

Hope for deliverance from the destructive effects of sin is rooted in the saving work of Jesus, who took on himself the punishment for what we did. In his Son, God hears our pleas for mercy and accepts them (v. 9). For those in Christ, regret never gets the last word.

God's Attributes

- fatherly
- forgiving
- just
- merciful

SING THE SONG

All our suffering, whether as the result of our sin or for reasons we do not know, is a form of God's discipline. In that regard, what does Hebrews 12:3–13 add to your understanding of God as he is revealed in Psalm 6?

Psalm

⤜ 7 ⤛

Safe in God

THEME

God defends his people and delivers them from evil.

HARMONY

Psalm 7 is a lament, a prayerful song that expresses perplexity, anguish, and even discouragement during times of overwhelming circumstances. Yet laments also reflect the confident hope of those who trust their compassionate and faithful God. The psalms of lament teach us that God welcomes boldness and honesty when we cry out to him, and we need not fear that he won't hear, because he has promised never to turn away from those who truly seek him. In Psalm 7, David's suffering was the result of hateful treatment by a man named Cush from the tribe of Benjamin.

SINGING IN TUNE

Every school yard has a bully, and no high school lacks a gaggle of mean girls. But bullying isn't confined to the under-eighteen set. There are bosses who bully employees, and nurses who bully patients; husbands who bully wives, and mothers who bully children. Whether weapons of words or fists, bullies crush those they target. But bullies are no match for God, which is why King David cried to God for help when he was mistreated (vv. 1–2). God knows when we are unjustly persecuted (vv. 3–5), and he is not indifferent to our plea for deliverance. In fact, he is angry when his children are threatened, and he will come to their aid

(vv. 6–7). We can count on it, because he knows who's who (vv. 8–9). Toward his own, he is a shield, but he is daily against those who oppose him (vv. 10–11). Bullies need him too, and unless they turn to him, they will be judged by God for the harm they do (vv. 12–13). If they do not repent, sooner or later their meanness will come back to bite them (vv. 15–16). God protects his own, and he doesn't sit back idly when others hurt them. He is always true to his character, which is why we can sing thanks like David did, even before we see the deliverance we so much need (v. 17). It will surely come.

MUSICAL NOTES

God's Grace

Every human being is accountable to God—both bullies and bullied—and in great need of the deliverance found only in Jesus Christ. Because Jesus was bullied on our behalf, the mistreated who trust in him are among those whom God promises to shield and deliver.

God's Attributes

- defending
- just
- protecting
- righteous

SING THE SONG

David asks God to judge him according to his righteousness (vv. 3–5), but this is no claim to sinlessness. His confidence in asking is that God is his shield (v. 10). Explain how Romans 5:1–5 helps you sing Psalm 7.

Psalm

❧ 8 ❧

Majesty

THEME

God's work in creation and the special status he gave to human beings is cause for rejoicing.

HARMONY

Many of the psalms were sung in celebration of God's greatness and the privileges that come to those who belong to him. These songs, called "praise psalms," were sung when Israel gathered for public worship. Psalm 8 harkens back to God's creation of the world in Genesis 1–2.

SINGING IN TUNE

People who don't know God consume creation for pleasure, pouring over vacation brochures and choosing the beach or mountain getaway package that most appeals. That's not how King David viewed it. He observed his natural surroundings with a God-shaped lens, which enabled him to comprehend that both majesty and mystery underlie its multifaceted diversity (vv. 1, 3). God's handiwork is unfathomable, whether moon and stars or the paradoxes he works in and among human beings (v. 2). The wonders of creation have been spread out before us not primarily for vacation fun but to inspire us with jaw-dropping awe over the fact that God cares most of all for human beings (vv. 4–5). David's song also includes praise that we were given the high privilege of reflecting his character—his "name"—to everything else he created (vv. 5–9).

MUSICAL NOTES

God's Grace

Since the time of the fall, we have failed to handle our God-given dominion as God intended. He called human beings to help creation flourish; instead we subjugate, enslave, and destroy. Our failure did not ruin God's plan, however, or cause him to reevaluate our privileged status. That's what David's praise points to, the One who exercised dominion with righteousness and merciful kindness, Jesus Christ. Although he was the Creator rather than one created, Jesus carried out what we have failed to do. That's why David can offer praise for God's original intention, despite our failure. The glory and honor we forfeited have been given to Jesus, and through him, God's intention for us has been restored.

God's Attributes

- caring
- creating
- glorious
- majestic
- strong

SING THE SONG

Explain how Genesis 2:1–3:15; Psalm 8; and Hebrews 2:5–9 are linked together.

Psalm

~ 9 ~

Our Stronghold

THEME

God is King over the whole world and everyone in it.

HARMONY

Many of the psalms were sung in celebration of God's greatness and the privileges that come to those who belong to him. These "praise psalms" were sung when Israel gathered for public worship and often included an invitation for outsiders to turn to God and worship him too. David, Israel's king, composed Psalm 9 to praise God as the great King over all.

SINGING IN TUNE

"I will . . . I will . . . I will . . . I will . . . " So declares David four times as he begins this song of confidence in the Lord (vv. 1–2). First, David will thank God, but this is no polite sort of thank you. His entire being overflows with it. Second, he will tell others about God's wonderful ways. Third, because of who God is, David is free to be happy. He makes a choice for gladness. Finally, he will sing praises to God not just for what God has done but primarily for who he is—all that makes up his "name." What makes this song so powerful is that David sang it while he was still in trouble, dealing with difficult circumstances and troubling people (v. 13). Praise songs are easily sung when some trial comes to an end, but in the midst of hard times our singing is not often as heartfelt. Not so with David. He had seen firsthand that God is strong when his people are

36

weak, and God will never leave his people alone to cope with their problems. Those who truly know God can't help but trust him (vv. 9–10, 12).

MUSICAL NOTES

God's Grace

As David praises God for who he is and thanks him for what he has already done and what he will certainly do, he adds a plea for help. In other words, David asks God to *do* what he has just praised God for *doing* (vv. 13–14). David isn't having sudden doubts, or fearing that God's help depends on his working a petition into his song. He is simply being real. Praise, thanks, and cries of longing can pour forth all at once when a relationship is real, and because of Jesus, sinful people can be real with a holy God.

God's Attributes

- faithful
- just
- kingly
- sustaining
- trustworthy

SING THE SONG

Describe how John 5:19–24; 17:1–2 and Colossians 2:8–9 reveal Jesus as the fulfillment of Psalm 9.

Psalm

10

Asking God Why

THEME

When evil presses in, God can be trusted to intervene because he cares for his people.

HARMONY

Psalm 10 is a lament composed by an unknown author, and it is viewed as a companion song to Psalm 9. Both psalms express the pain of overwhelming circumstances. Yet they also reflect the confident hope of those who trust God as the great eternal King. The psalms of lament teach us that God welcomes boldness and honesty when we cry out to him, and we need not fear that he won't hear, because he has promised never to turn away from those who truly seek him.

SINGING IN TUNE

Why, O Lord? We are cautioned against asking God to explain himself, and for good reason. He owes us no explanation for what he does. And when the heart behind our *why* is arrogant and demanding, we are unlikely to receive a satisfactory answer. But the psalmist's *why* is not of that sort. He is perplexed at God's ways, and he wants to understand so that his trust won't be shaken. What he sees going on around him— the wicked crushing the weak—doesn't seem to match what he knows of God's justice, compassion, and power (vv. 1–10). In other words, the psalmist is praying his perplexity. Asking why in this way is not a demand; it's an act of drawing near. Jesus put it this way: "Everyone who asks receives, and the one who seeks finds, and to the one who knocks it will be opened" (Matt. 7:8). The psalmist asked, and he received a reminder that God is the eternal King who hears the cries of the oppressed and does something about it. The psalmist sought, and he found renewed confidence in the father-heart of God. The psalmist knocked, and his prayer changed from perplexed lament to confident petition (vv. 12–18).

MUSICAL NOTES

God's Grace

From the psalmist we learn that God delights in the searching of an honest heart, and for that reason, we are free to sing our *why* songs to God. "Humble yourselves, therefore, under the mighty hand of God so that at the proper time he may exalt you, casting all your anxieties on him, because he cares for you" (1 Pet. 5:6–7).

God's Attributes

- defending
- just
- listening
- near
- protecting
- righteous

SING THE SONG

Consider which of your own *why* questions are answered in 1 Peter 4:12–19.

Psalm

~~ 11 ~~

Secure Foundations

THEME

Troubles come with a choice: we can either run away in fear or trust in the righteous and good character of the Lord.

HARMONY

Psalm 11 was composed by David to express confidence in God. God's people sang psalms of confidence during seasons of persecution or other kinds of suffering.

SINGING IN TUNE

Running from trouble is a wise move unless, of course, our flight is motivated by panic. Actions that arise from panic are never the outworking of faith. The safest course, no matter the difficulty, is to run to the Lord before we run anywhere else. That's what David did, and it enabled him to grapple with his fear (v. 1). Panic skews our perspective—about everything—whereas resting in the Lord brings discernment. Safe in God's care, David could face the crisis and the very real threat confronting him (vv. 2–3). Running to God rather than away gave David a big-picture glimpse of God's good purposes in hardships—to refine the faith of his people. God tests the righteous, which is an act of love, but he hates those who stubbornly set their hearts against him (v. 5). God's hatred is different from human hatred, which springs from sin and powerful emotions. God's hatred arises from his character—he is so perfectly righteous, holy, and just that he simply cannot tolerate evil.

MUSICAL NOTES

God's Grace

There are times when we hear what David heard: "If the foundations are destroyed, what can the righteous do?" (v. 3). But there is no need to panic. By resting in the Lord rather than running from him to some nearby quick fix of available comfort, we find that we already have the answer to that question. In David's day, God's people found security in the protective presence of God in Jerusalem, most fully in the sanctuary of God's house. Today, we have even more reason to feel secure, because in Christ we have become part of the very temple itself as "members of the household of God" (Eph. 2:19).

God's Attributes

- holy
- protecting
- purifying
- ruling

SING THE SONG

Drawing from 1 Corinthians 3:11; Ephesians 2:19–22; and 2 Timothy 2:16–19, explain how you would answer David's question in verse 3.

$\mathcal{P}_{salm}$

❧❧ 12 ❧❧

Our Only Refuge

THEME

When we are dominated or oppressed by arrogant unbelievers, we can appeal to God for help and call to mind his never-failing justice.

HARMONY

Psalm 12 is a lament that was composed by David for the whole community to sing. Laments express perplexity, anguish, and sometimes even discouragement during times of overwhelming circumstances. Yet they also reflect the confident hope of those who trust their compassionate and faithful God. The psalms of lament teach us that God welcomes boldness and honesty when we cry out to him, and we need not fear that he won't hear, because he has promised never to turn away from those who truly seek him.

SINGING IN TUNE

Discouragement blinds us to reality. It makes everything look worse than it actually is. That's where David is when he begins his song. Evildoers have worked so much damage that glimpses of goodness are hard to find (vv. 1–2). Especially burdensome is the fact that those perpetrating the evil have at least some measure of authority, and they are arrogantly using their position to take advantage of the poor (v. 5). David sets these injustices before the Lord, and as he does, his discouragement is replaced with hope. By taking his downcast mood to the Lord in prayer, he is reminded that God has a special heart for the disadvantaged, and therefore, deliverance is sure to come (vv. 5, 7). By the end of his prayer, David's discouragement has been replaced by the hope that comes from trusting that God is always true to his character and will never fail to keep his promises (v. 6).

MUSICAL NOTES

God's Grace

We can sing with confidence in our security, even when the safety God promises does not include a peaceful society that allows us to live out the American dream in ease and comfort. We know for sure that his promise of safety does include what we most need—rescue from sin and all the forces of evil that rage against us. "You, O LORD, will keep them," David sings; "you will guard us . . . forever" (vv. 7–8). David looked forward to eternal deliverance, but we look back upon it. It is finished. In Christ we have been rescued from evil and set in the safety we need most of all.

God's Attributes

- compassionate
- faithful
- just
- protecting

SING THE SONG

Consider how John 17:1–26 reveals the fulfillment of Psalm 12.

$\mathcal{P}\!\mathit{salm}$

❧ 13 ❧

Waiting

THEME

When long-endured difficulties take a toll, we can turn to God for a renewal of hope.

HARMONY

Psalm 13 is a lament composed by David. Laments express perplexity, anguish, and even discouragement during times of overwhelming circumstances. Yet they also reflect the confident hope of those who trust their compassionate and faithful God. The psalms of lament teach us that God welcomes boldness and honesty when we cry out to him. We need not fear that he won't hear, because he has promised never to turn away from those who truly seek him.

SINGING IN TUNE

David is soul weary. He cannot escape his difficulty, and the sorrow that attends it smothers his enthusiasm for day-to-day life (vv. 1–2). Especially discouraging is that God seems distant and unconcerned. Why won't he intervene to help? So David pleads not only for deliverance from his difficulty but, even more, for an indicator that God hasn't abandoned him. He recognizes that his troubles have made him lonely for God himself (vv. 3–4). As David looks to the Lord, his depression lifts and his heart is encouraged, even though his circumstances haven't yet changed. He is no longer weary because God's love for him is bigger than the source of his heartache, and he is confident that in time to come, he will sing yet another song of God's deliverance (vv. 5–6).

MUSICAL NOTES
God's Grace
Through David's song, we are given a theology of waiting. During prolonged seasons of difficulty, God invites us to spread our trouble before him, along with our weariness in trying to cope. He welcomes our cries for relief, both spiritually and circumstantially. When we are suffering, our primary concern is so often simply relief from trouble, but God is so much more concerned with what he accomplishes in us while we wait. "From of old no one has heard or perceived by the ear, no eye has seen a God besides you, who acts for those who wait for him" (Isa. 64:4).

God's Attributes
- comforting
- faithful
- patient
- providing
- trustworthy

SING THE SONG
Set forth a "theology of waiting" from Scripture. Here are some passages to get you started: Isaiah 30:18; 40:28–31; 64:4; Lamentations 3:25; Romans 8:18–25; James 5:7–11; 2 Peter 3:11–13.

Psalm

ᵈ᪻᪻᪻ 14 ᪻᪻᪻

The Heart of a Fool

THEME

Everyone rejects God and pursues sin, yet in God there is hope for salvation.

HARMONY

Psalm 14 is a lament composed by David for the entire believing community to sing together. Laments express perplexity and anguish, yet they also reflect the confident hope of those who trust a faithful God. The psalms of lament teach us that God welcomes boldness and honesty when we cry out to him, and we need not fear that he won't hear, because he has promised never to turn away from those who truly seek him.

SINGING IN TUNE

The wise are those who set their heart on the Lord, so it stands to reason that the opposite is just as true—fools are those who reject God and deny that he even exists. That's how David begins this song, but he takes it a step further by giving us God's perspective on the human heart: "They have all turned aside; together they have become corrupt" (v. 3). It's a grim picture. From God's standpoint, no one is wise. "There is no one who does good, not even one" (v. 3). It began at the fall, when Adam and Eve turned away from God, and rejecting him has been the default mode of everyone ever since. Left to ourselves, we are doomed, but in God there is hope. Only God can deliver us from the messes of our own making, and David prays for that salvation, which restores and rejoices (v. 7).

MUSICAL NOTES
God's Grace

No one does good, not even one—except for Jesus. Those who put their faith in his goodness are counted righteous, and those who call on him know God as their refuge from all the horrible effects of sin—both what they do and what gets done to them by others (vv. 4–6). David sang of the day when God would heap blessings on his people (v. 7), but we can sing because we live in that day now.

God's Attributes

- all-knowing
- delivering
- righteous
- saving

SING THE SONG

Read Romans 3:9–26 and explain the truth Paul is proclaiming there, where he quotes Psalm 14.

Psalm

✤ 15 ✤

Portrait of a Disciple

THEME

God's standards of righteousness are high and holy.

HARMONY

"Who shall dwell on [God's] holy hill?" asks David (v. 1). The holy hill is Zion, the mountain in Jerusalem where the temple was built. The temple was the special place where God revealed his presence, protection, and power to his people. This special gathering place was a shadow of a greater temple to come. It came in the form of a person, Jesus Christ, and all those united to him by faith become part of a spiritual temple, the church. The big picture of the temple in Scripture is God and man dwelling together in close fellowship.

SINGING IN TUNE

Who is qualified to enjoy God's presence and true fellowship with God's people? David begins with that question to get people thinking about what most pleases God (v. 1), and then he sets forth the criteria. God is pleased by those who obey his commands, speak only truth, put others ahead of themselves, honor fellow believers, and care for the poor (vv. 2–5). At the end, it seems that David leaves us hanging—who can measure up to this? We have to realize that the foundation of his song is faith—the only thing that has ever justified anyone. People may practice the qualifications David lists, but without faith the motivation is self-serving and does not lead to God's holy hill. Only faith breeds the desire to please God, no matter how imperfectly lived out, and only faith takes us there.

MUSICAL NOTES

God's Grace

Holiness is necessary for those who want to be numbered among God's people, but no one lives up to it. We do unholy things, and even the intentions of our hearts are tainted by sin. Only one person has ever met the requirements of Psalm 15—Jesus. He always spoke the truth, never did evil, and constantly put others first, and he did all that on our behalf because we simply cannot. In union with him, although we are still sinners, we already reside on God's holy hill.

God's Attributes

- holy
- relational
- righteous

SING THE SONG

Explain how Ephesians 2:13–22 fulfills Psalm 15.

Psalm

~ 16 ~

A Rich Inheritance

THEME

Trust in God's care and provision is the key to rest and contentment.

HARMONY

David composed Psalm 16 as a song of trust.

SINGING IN TUNE

Through many harrowing experiences, David had learned that contentment—the deep, lasting kind—comes only to those who anchor their lives in God. When times are good, God is the reason (v. 2). God oversees the details of his people's lives, from the places they live to the companions they have. And he loves to bless his people in tangible, practical ways. David calls these blessings "pleasant places" and "a beautiful inheritance" (vv. 5–6). That's how we experience life when God is at the center of it, and it doesn't evaporate in the hard times. When troubles come, we discover that God is ever present to guide us, and in the process he deepens our capacity to enjoy him and his ways even more fully (v. 11).

MUSICAL NOTES

God's Grace

God provides for us in the present and preserves us for ongoing, everlasting blessings, all of which come to us through the death and resurrection of Jesus. In union with him, we share David's confidence in declaring,

"The lines have fallen for me in pleasant places; indeed, I have a beautiful inheritance" (v. 6). In the ups and downs of each day, in small irritations or major crises—not just "some day," but right now—are contentment, joy, and pleasures that will never disappoint (v. 11). When Christ is our portion, every blessing named in Psalm 16 is ours to enjoy.

God's Attributes
- delighting
- guiding
- life-giving
- protecting
- providing
- saving

SING THE SONG

Explain how the words of Peter (Acts 2:22–31) and Paul (Acts 13:32–39) deepen your understanding of Psalm 16.

Psalm

✣ 17 ✣

The Apple of God's Eye

THEME

God can be trusted to protect and provide for his people because he loves them.

HARMONY

Psalm 17 is a lament, a prayerful song that expresses perplexity, anguish, and even discouragement during times of overwhelming circumstances. Laments also reflect the confident hope of those who trust their compassionate and faithful God. The psalms of lament teach us that God welcomes boldness and honesty when we cry out to him. We need not fear that he won't hear, because he has promised never to turn away from those who truly seek him. Psalm 17 was composed by David while he was experiencing unjust treatment.

SINGING IN TUNE

Suffering unjustly at the hands of evildoers, David calls on God for help, and he is confident that God will answer him because he knows he is cherished in God's eyes (vv. 1–7). David wants to see God's protective love at work, keeping him safe from those who think nothing of trampling on others to get all they can from this life. "Keep me as the apple of your eye," David prays (v. 8). That expression for intense love didn't originate with Hallmark but with Moses. It's how he described God's hovering, protective care for his people whenever danger threatened

(Deut. 32:10). It's what it means to be cherished. Amazing as it seems, God's people are the apple of his eye, and for that reason we can sing this song when worldly scorn is aimed our way and our faith proves personally costly. One way or another, sooner or later, God always delivers his people. At times he intervenes to stop evil from harming our lives and relationships, and at other times his deliverance awaits a future day. Either way, true satisfaction is found in the Lord and his ways (v. 15).

MUSICAL NOTES

God's Grace

"From your presence let my vindication come!" David prayed (v. 2), and God answered him. Even so, the fullest answer wouldn't come for a thousand more years. It was met in David's descendant Jesus, who was treated more unjustly than David ever was. The sinless Jesus was crucified and buried in a tomb, but God raised him from the dead. Jesus is now enthroned as King forever, fully vindicated. In union with him, we can sing David's song with confidence, because our life is "hidden with Christ in God" (Col. 3:3).

God's Attributes

- just
- listening
- loving
- protecting
- righteous
- satisfying

SING THE SONG

Explain how Romans 8:31–39 serves as a companion passage to Psalm 17.

Psalm

❧ 18 ❧

Our Great Deliverer

THEME

God shows himself powerful and faithful on behalf of those who love him.

HARMONY

God appointed a line of kings, beginning with David, to lead his people in his ways. And God promised that through this line would come his greatest blessings (see 2 Sam. 7:12–17). Sure enough, when the kings served faithfully, all the people were blessed. But ultimately they were all failures in faithfulness—every last one—and all God's people suffered for it. Even so, some of the psalms, like Psalm 18, are songs of rejoicing about the king, which can mean only one thing—despite the royal failures in the psalmist's days, there was still hope. The ideal King was still to come. Humans—even kings—fail, but God does not. He always keeps his promises. Psalms that rejoice in the king are called "royal psalms."

SINGING IN TUNE

David originally composed this song to thank God for delivering him from great personal trouble and protecting him to serve as king of God's people (2 Samuel 22). As a result, it became a national hymn for singing in public worship. Even then, however, the pronoun "I" in the song wasn't changed to "we." God cares that every one of his people knows him personally as a rock, a fortress, and a shield. He want us to love him, not because he gives us strength but because he *is* our strength (vv. 1–2).

Walking in God's ways enabled David to know and experience the wonders of God's character (vv. 20–24). He hadn't earned God's favor—far from it! After all, David's sins were public record. Yet he walked in God's ways by confessing those sins, which is why he could sing about his righteousness (v. 20). We can sing these words with even more joy than David because we know that the blamelessness of Christ has covered our sins. The Lord reveals himself to humble people—those who see their need of him—and he delights to rescue them (v. 27). For the humble, God turns darkness into light and weakness into strength (vv. 28–29).

MUSICAL NOTES

God's Grace

God invites the prayers of the weak and desperate. As we sing this song during our low moments and days, we will hear in our hearts and know in our troubles the promise of Jesus: "'My grace is sufficient for you, for my power is made perfect in weakness.' Therefore I will boast all the more gladly of my weaknesses, so that the power of Christ may rest upon me" (2 Cor. 12:9).

God's Attributes

- delivering
- faithful
- just
- listening
- loving
- powerful
- rescuing
- saving

SING THE SONG

Compile a two-column list from all David says about the Lord in Psalm 18. On one side, list everything God is, and on the other side list all the things God does.

Psalm

❧ 19 ❦

God Wants to Be Known

THEME

God draws near and makes himself known through the things he has created and even more fully in his Word.

HARMONY

David composed Psalm 19 for God's people to sing as they rejoiced in the ways God reveals himself.

SINGING IN TUNE

The gold and purple dance of the sun as it leads day into night and back again—the heavens indeed declare the glory of God (v. 1). God reveals himself to us in the intricate mystery of moon and stars and patterns of clouds. Do we notice, or does self-interest cause us to miss it? So long as we live, his creativity is there to see, fresh and new, every day. The glory of the heavens, however, gives just a glimpse. His Word, the Bible, is a fuller revelation and even more powerful. His Word revives us, rejoices our heart, enlightens our mind, makes us wise, and leads to blessing (vv. 7–11). Those who get a taste of its riches know its blessings and will therefore pray for help never to wander from its course (vv. 12–13).

MUSICAL NOTES

God's Grace

The happenings in the sky are, for us, too often nothing more than a wardrobe guide. But in all the vastness above us, God gives us daily opportunity to behold his power and creative beauty with no effort on our part except to look up. Better still is all we learn of him through his Word. The Bible is like no other book—it's living and active, and it transforms those who study it. God's fullest revelation is unquestionably his living Word—Jesus Christ. "He is the radiance of the glory of God and the exact imprint of his nature" (Heb. 1:3).

God's Attributes

- knowable
- majestic
- powerful
- redeeming

SING THE SONG

Meditate on Hebrews 4:12.

Psalm

❧ 20 ☙

How Blessings Come

THEME

The welfare of God's people is tied to the success of God's appointed king.

HARMONY

Psalms 20 and 21 form a pair. Psalm 20 is a prayer for blessing on King David as he leads God's people, and Psalm 21 praises and thanks God for answering that prayer. God appointed a line of kings, beginning with David, to lead his people in his ways. And God promised that through this line would come his greatest blessings (see 2 Sam. 7:12–17). That's why all God's people prayed eagerly for the welfare of the king—when he prospered, so would they. God's promise underlies Psalm 20, which is why it is called a "royal psalm."

SINGING IN TUNE

Those gathered together for worship direct their song to the king himself, and they sing of the specific ways they pray for him. They ask God to answer the king's prayers, protect him as he leads, and guard him with spiritual health. They know that their well-being is linked to David's (vv. 1–5). Then they voice their confidence that God will answer and will keep his promise to bless the king and all who serve him. Ultimately, their confidence isn't in David; it's in God himself. He is the One they trust (vv. 6–9). Psalm 20 helps us shift our prayer focus higher than just the day-to-day things we hope God will do in our lives. Of course we pray about our personal concerns—God welcomes these. But if that's our primary focus, we are missing out on prayerful participation in God's big-picture plan, which is to bless the entire world through King Jesus.

MUSICAL NOTES

God's Grace

As Israel rejoiced in the blessings of King David, so we rejoice in the blessings of the King of kings, Jesus. In him we are brought near to God and saved from every danger. And by his name we are assured that God will always answer when we call.

God's Attributes

- delivering
- listening
- powerful
- saving

SING THE SONG

Consider how John 14:12–14 helps you apply Psalm 20.

Psalm

～〉〉～ 21 ～〈〈～

God Answers Prayer

THEME

God's answers to his people's prayers exceed their expectations.

HARMONY

Psalms 20 and 21 form a pair. Psalm 20 is a prayer for blessing on King David as he leads God's people, and Psalm 21 praises and thanks God for answering that prayer. God had promised to bless his people through David as king (see 2 Sam. 7:12–17). That's why they prayed eagerly for the king's welfare—when he prospered, so would they. God's promise to bless the people through their king underlies Psalm 21, which is why it is called a "royal psalm."

SINGING IN TUNE

David's prayer was answered, and all the people rejoiced. God delights to listen to the prayers of his people, and he takes pleasure in their joy when the answer comes. The answer David received exceeded the desire of his heart (v. 2). He had expressed his longing to build a house for God (2 Sam. 7:1–29), but God's answer was far greater than stones and mortar. Through the Lord's enabling, David built an eternal dynasty, culminating in his descendant Jesus Christ. During his reign, David's source of joy was the Lord himself, and his confidence in the Lord's love for him gave him the stability to rule God's people and conquer all his enemies (vv. 7–13).

MUSICAL NOTES

God's Grace

As God's people today, we can sing David's song even more joyfully as subjects of King Jesus, whose benefits flow down on us. In and through him, we have confidence that God hears—and answers—all our prayers. In King Jesus, we have "length of days forever and ever" (v. 4). In this King we are met with rich blessings (v. 3). In him we are able to defeat our enemies of sin and Satan (vv. 11–12). In this King we find all our heart's desire (v. 2).

God's Attributes

- answering
- guiding
- listening
- providing
- saving
- supplying

SING THE SONG

Consider how Ephesians 3:14–21 and Philippians 4:4–7 guide you in applying Psalm 21 to your life.

Psalm

⤖ 22 ⬿

Never Forsaken

THEME

God does not abandon his people when they suffer.

HARMONY

Psalm 22 is an anguished lament that expresses both the reality of pain in hardship and the hope that comes through trusting a faithful God. The psalms of lament teach us that God welcomes boldness and honesty when we cry out to him, and we need not fear that he won't hear, because he has promised never to turn away from those who truly seek him.

SINGING IN TUNE

Sometimes—often during the worst crises—God seems absent. If he is all he has promised to be for his people, why is he hard to find when we need him most? Not only does he allow our trouble to continue (and sometimes worsen), but he also seems to hide from us. We find no comfort when we cry out, and he provides no evidence that he cares about our plight. That's where David found himself. He felt forsaken by God, and his prayers brought no sweet peace to give him hope (vv. 1–2). Hopeless though he felt, he clung to his faith, reminding himself of God's deliverances in times past (v. 4) and of the lifelong relationship he'd enjoyed with the Lord (v. 10). We don't know exactly what David's trouble was in this situation, but we do know that it involved people who sought to harm him and shake up his faith (vv. 7–8, 12–13). Such is the case with our greatest enemies too. In fact, anyone or anything that seeks to convince us that trusting in God is fruitless is an enemy. And when such enemies gain a foothold, God seems farther away than ever, and we are overcome with mental, spiritual, and sometimes physical weakness (vv. 14–18). Despite all this, David doesn't give up. He doesn't turn elsewhere for help. He perseveres in prayer, pleading for rescue and for a sense of God's nearness once again (v. 11). As he does, his confidence is restored, and he sings of future days when his cries of angst will instead be joyful testimony and cries of praise (vv. 22–24).

MUSICAL NOTES

God's Grace

Even when God seems absent, he is not. And when he seems callous to our cries, he is working out his answer even then. Of this we can be confident because of the One he did forsake, the One whose cries he turned away from. It was Jesus, not David, whose hands and feet were really and truly pierced and whose suffering was made into sport. God didn't rescue his Son; he let him suffer in order to rescue us. That's why, when our enemies are doing their worst and God seems most absent, we can still rejoice. "It shall be told of the Lord to the coming generation; they shall come and proclaim his righteousness to a people yet unborn, that he has done it" (vv. 30–31).

God's Attributes

- ever-present
- ruling
- saving

SING THE SONG

Make note of all the ways in which Matthew 27 echoes Psalm 22.

Psalm

✺ 23 ✺

Our Shepherd

THEME

God watches over his people and guides the course of their individual lives.

HARMONY

David composed Psalm 23 to inspire confidence in the Lord's care.

SINGING IN TUNE

What has become a most beloved psalm was crafted from David's past. Before his royal calling, David was a shepherd of sheep, and he drew from his memories of those days to describe all he had learned about God's character. In the same way, we can look back on what God has brought us through—the good times and the bad—and recount all he has taught us about himself and how, through it all, he grew our walk with him and imparted hope for the future. Psalm 23 is so loved because it's not just David's experience; it's ours too. From sunup to sundown, a shepherd cares for the needs of sheep, and in his shepherding role, David learned that this is no passive job. A shepherd doesn't sit in the grass and yell commands to keep the sheep on track; he undertakes to get them to places where the food is nutritious and chaos doesn't dominate (vv. 1–3). It is necessary sometimes for a shepherd to take his sheep through rough terrain, but he never sends them there alone. Sheep cannot foresee danger, and if left to themselves, they are likely to either run away in fear or be killed along the way. So the shepherd leads them, and when they begin to stray, he nudges with his rod and keeps them on course with the crook of his staff (v. 4), guiding them in good ways and covering them with compassion until they are finally home (vv. 5–6).

MUSICAL NOTES

God's Grace

Jesus is the Good Shepherd who not only guides his sheep but also laid down his life to save them. He knows each one of his sheep by name, and he is able to protect them from harm. In Jesus, God fulfilled his promise: "I myself will be the shepherd of my sheep, and I myself will make them lie down, declares the Lord God. I will seek the lost, and I will bring back the strayed, and I will bind up the injured, and I will strengthen the weak, and the fat and the strong I will destroy. I will feed them in justice" (Ezek. 34:15–16).

God's Attributes

- following
- guiding
- leading
- protecting
- providing

SING THE SONG

Describe what John 10:11–15; Hebrews 13:20–21; 1 Peter 2:24–25; and Revelation 7:13–17 add to your understanding of our Great Shepherd.

Psalm

❧ 24 ❧

Our Creator King

THEME

God saves those who truly seek him.

HARMONY

Psalm 24 was sung during public worship, perhaps when the people wanted to remember the joyful occasion of David bringing the ark of the Lord into Jerusalem (see 2 Samuel 6 for background).

SINGING IN TUNE

As Creator and sustainer of everything, God is worthy of worship (vv. 1–2), and as his people ponder his greatness, they are humbled (v. 3). So pure is the Lord that only holy people can dwell with him and receive his special blessings. God wants not only righteous deeds but also pure hearts (vv. 4–5). Were it not for his mercy, no one could qualify, but in his kindness he brings in all who truly seek him, who receive his righteousness as a gift (vv. 5–6). True seekers are characterized by joy because they delight in God's presence and in proclaiming his glory in the company of other believers (vv. 7–10).

MUSICAL NOTES

God's Grace

Jesus is the only one who lived life with clean hands and a pure heart. He met all God's conditions of righteousness for us because we do not.

Indeed we *cannot*. He did it for us, in our place. "Since we have confidence to enter the holy places by the blood of Jesus, by the new and living way that he opened for us . . . , let us draw near with a true heart in full assurance of faith" (Heb. 10:19–22).

God's Attributes
- blessing
- creating
- purifying
- sustaining

SING THE SONG
Explain how James 4:7–10 helps you apply Psalm 24.

Psalm

❧ 25 ❧

Our Teacher

THEME

God teaches and guides those who seek his paths.

HARMONY

David composed Psalm 25 as a lament. Laments express perplexity, anguish, and even discouragement during times of overwhelming circumstances, and they teach us that God welcomes boldness and honesty when we cry out to him. Some laments include an acknowledgment of sin, as we find here in Psalm 25. These songs remind us that God has promised never to turn away from those who truly seek him.

SINGING IN TUNE

Small-scale stress or crushing crisis—we face a crossroads with each one. Sin or obedience? God's way or the world's? We choose our path not just once but again and again, every hour of every day. Those who trust in the Lord, as David did, turn to the Lord for help (vv. 1–3). Even so, choosing that path is a battle sometimes, so David prays for help to choose rightly, whatever it takes: *"Make me* to know your ways, O LORD" (v. 4). Guilt doesn't hinder David's prayer for guidance, because God doesn't withhold guidance from sinners (vv. 6–8, 11). Although sinlessness isn't required, humility is—a willingness to walk wherever God leads (vv. 9, 12). As we lift our eyes off our troubles—and off ourselves—and fix our focus on God, we find ourselves desiring God's paths. Even then, we are daily in need of his help. Seeking him, even for the enabling to keep on seeking, is what it means to "fear" the Lord (vv. 12–14), and as we do, our choices become clear (vv. 12–13). Best of all, God gives himself to those who cling to him (v. 14), and he is faithful to remove whatever hinders them along the way (vv. 16–22).

MUSICAL NOTES

God's Grace

God teaches and guides sinners not because we deserve it, but because he is good. In fact, everything he does for us springs from his goodness, most especially our salvation. "For while we were still weak, at the right time Christ died for the ungodly. For one will scarcely die for a righteous person—though perhaps for a good person one would dare even to die— but God shows his love for us in that while we were still sinners, Christ died for us" (Rom. 5:6–8).

God's Attributes

- befriending
- delivering
- forgiving
- leading
- loving
- redeeming
- teaching

SING THE SONG

Make application of Psalm 25 from Romans 12:1–2.

Psalm

❦ 26 ❦

Walking with the Lord

THEME

Walking in God's ways brings safety and stability.

HARMONY

God's people sang some of the psalms as they entered the temple for worship. Psalm 26 may have been one such song, because it leads those who sing it to reflect on the state of their hearts as they come into the Lord's presence.

SINGING IN TUNE

Loyalty to the Lord is the fruit of love for the Lord. Of course, we can do right things, but done without love, the primary motivation is merely self-improvement. God offers his heart to us and with it the privilege of a real love relationship, the kind that goes both ways. He actually takes the initiative; we need only respond. David shows us what this reciprocal relationship looks like. He walked uprightly with God, but that doesn't mean he was sinless; he knew he was not. But by living close to God—trusting him and keeping him always in view—the passion of David's heart and the path of his life were clearly defined (vv. 1–3). Spiritual health is evidenced by how we safeguard it, and that includes being careful about the company we keep (vv. 4–5), forsaking known sin (v. 6), telling others about God's goodness (v. 7), gathering for worship with other believers (v. 8), and praying for spiritual protection (vv. 9–11). The fruit of such godly living is peace and stability (v. 12).

MUSICAL NOTES
God's Grace
We cannot walk in God's way by willpower alone. The enabling we need comes only from God himself. Like David, we need God's gracious redemption, which he has provided through his Son "in order that, just as Christ was raised from the dead by the glory of the Father, we too might walk in newness of life" (Rom. 6:4).

God's Attributes
- establishing
- forgiving
- redeeming
- testing
- vindicating

SING THE SONG
Consider how 2 Peter 1:3–8 enables you to apply Psalm 26.

Psalm

❦ 27 ❦

The Lord Our Light

THEME

Nothing and no one can harm those who shelter under the protection of God.

HARMONY

Psalm 27 was composed by David to both express and deepen trust in the Lord.

SINGING IN TUNE

Suburbs or city, at home or at work, in love or alone—no matter where we live or what we do—life is beyond our control. So we can hide in fear, or we can hide in the Lord, which was David's choice (v. 1). Bad things happen even to God's people, but there is nothing to fear because God protects his own (v. 5). David longed for deliverance from difficulty, but even more, he longed to know God and experience the pleasure of his presence (v. 4). And abiding in God gave him an accurate perspective of his troubles (v. 6). Abiding brings clarity—whatever comes, God will either avert the trouble, or he will carry us through it. Rejection by a loved one is among the worst of pains, but God will never cast off those who love him (v. 10). Instead, he will guide them into new and more stable paths (vv. 11–12). Hiding in the Lord includes waiting for him to act, and we can wait with hope when we know the good character of the God we're hiding in. That's how David waited—because he believed that

God would provide an answer to his problem (vv. 13–14). The Lord our God is well worth waiting for.

MUSICAL NOTES

God's Grace

In Jesus, every blessing David sings of in Psalm 27 is ours for the asking. He is our light and salvation and our stronghold in times of trouble. He conquers our sin and the forces of evil aligned against us. He has assured us a home with him forever, and he will get us there safely. He will never cast us off. When we abide in him, we rest in confidence because to us he says, "Let not your hearts be troubled, neither let them be afraid" (John 14:27).

God's Attributes

- hope-giving
- illuminating
- loving
- protecting
- providing
- revealing
- saving

SING THE SONG

Describe how John 15:1–10 enriches the revelation of God's character that's given to us in Psalm 27.

Psalm

·≫ 28 ≪·

Strength, Shield, and Shepherd

THEME

God hears and answers the bold prayers of those who love and trust him.

HARMONY

Psalm 28 is a lament that expresses desperation but also confident hope for deliverance. Included in David's song is a prayer for the destruction of his tormentors. This was no personal vendetta on David's part; psalms that include these requests are motivated by a desire for the triumph of righteousness over evil. In praying this way, David was upholding God's just and holy character.

SINGING IN TUNE

A cry for help. At times that's the only way we can pray. Some trouble we've been dealing with takes a turn for the worse, or a brand-new crisis breaks over our life in the course of a single day, an hour, a phone call. When that happens, when we are suddenly and utterly overwhelmed, God is there. Our new crisis is not new to God, so we can simply cry out for help. That's exactly what David does as he prays for deliverance and for a divinely imposed barrier on the evil coming against him (vv. 1–5). Even before the answer comes, David is confident that God has heard him and will provide the deliverance he needs, because God is the protector of his people (vv. 6–9).

MUSICAL NOTES

God's Grace

David's prayer for God's people, "Be their shepherd and carry them forever" (v. 9), has been fully and finally answered in the Good Shepherd, Jesus Christ, who laid down his life for his sheep (John 10:11). In his care, we are safe. "Now may the God of peace who brought again from the dead our Lord Jesus, the great shepherd of the sheep, by the blood of the eternal covenant, equip you with everything good that you may do his will, working in us that which is pleasing in his sight, through Jesus Christ, to whom be glory forever and ever. Amen" (Heb. 13:20–21).

God's Attributes

- helping
- listening
- saving
- shepherding

SING THE SONG

Note the particular aspects of John 14:12–14 and Hebrews 4:14–16 that increase your confidence in prayer.

Psalm

❧ 29 ☙

Lord of the Storm

THEME

The God who controls the workings of the universe is able to supply strength to his people.

HARMONY

Many of the psalms were composed to celebrate God's greatness and the privileges that come to those who belong to him. These songs, called "praise psalms," were sung when Israel gathered for public worship, and within many of them there is an invitation for outsiders to turn to God and worship him too. David composed Psalm 29 as he reflected on God's majestic power over a thunderstorm.

SINGING IN TUNE

God has infinite ways of making himself known. The universe is his stage, and all its ever-changing features are his props. He delights to reveal himself; he wants us to know him in all his multifaceted wonder. *Majesty* is one of those facets—his great splendor and royal bearing. It comes and takes our breath away in the terror of a violent thunderstorm (vv. 3–4) or in the rise of the evening star in a clear, purple twilight. It washes over us when we stand on the edge of the shore and watch the breakers crash, rolling in and out and back again. It awes us when it appears in the talents of human beings, in artistic masterpieces and architectural marvels. God speaks his majesty to all his creation (v. 9). God's majesty in the world around us is merely a glimpse of his royal bearing, but it points to where it is revealed most fully—in the King of kings, Jesus Christ, who reigns now and will retain his royal status forever (v. 10). He is majesty made flesh, and as King he bequeaths to his subjects strength and peace (v. 11).

MUSICAL NOTES

God's Grace

The Lord who creates storms can walk upon them or quiet them at will, and he does so for his people when they cry out to him for rescue. Storms may rage, but we need not doubt his care, even when the storm intensifies. He is there, and we simply wait until he stops the waves with his word—"Peace! Be still" (Mark 4:39).

God's Attributes

- majestic
- peace-giving
- powerful
- rescuing

SING THE SONG

Describe how Psalm 29 together with Colossians 1:15–20 enriches your understanding of God.

Psalm

🌿 30 🌿

Joy Comes with the Morning

THEME

God is faithful to bless his people and keep them in his love.

HARMONY

David composed Psalm 30 as he thought ahead to the temple that would be built in Jerusalem. A day would come when God's people would gather there for worship, and they would sing this song in thanksgiving.

SINGING IN TUNE

David's walk with the Lord, which he describes in this song, is the walk of every one of God's children. The Lord preserves us from our foes, most especially sin and Satan. He helps and heals, restores and saves (vv. 1–3). As David reflects on God's ways with him, he breaks into praise and thanksgiving (v. 4). God doesn't shield his people from sorrow or from all the consequences of their sin, and sometimes he allows painful trials to linger, but sooner or later, one way or another, he turns each one into joy (v. 5). God in his faithfulness hinders our self-sufficiency, even by hiding a sense of his presence or his protecting hand at times (vv. 6–7). In that way we are drawn back to him in conscious dependence, and our joy in him is renewed (vv. 8–12).

MUSICAL NOTES

God's Grace

God momentarily hid his face from David, but he never abandoned him. He was close beside him all along. Even so, David's experience was awful.

Yet it was nothing compared to Jesus's separation from God during his crucifixion. In agony Jesus cried, "My God, my God, why have you forsaken me?" (Matt. 27:46). David only felt forsaken, but Jesus actually was. And because of that, we never will be. The most joyful morning in all of history came three days later, when God raised Jesus from the dead, after which he ascended back into the presence of his Father. His resurrection is the guarantee that our nights of weeping will end in morning joy.

God's Attributes
- delivering
- healing
- joy-giving
- restoring
- saving

SING THE SONG

Describe what 2 Corinthians 12:1–10 adds to your understanding of the Lord as he is presented in Psalm 30.

Psalm

❧ 31 ❧

Abundant Goodness

THEME

God restores those worn out by sin and sorrow.

HARMONY

Psalm 31 is a lament composed by David. Laments express freely the emotional pain that accompanies troubling circumstances, yet they also reflect hope in a promise-keeping God. Included in David's song here is a prayer for the downfall of his enemies. Revenge wasn't his motive; he yearned to see a visible display of righteousness triumphing over evil. The psalms of lament teach us that God welcomes boldness and honesty when we cry out to him. We need not fear that he won't hear, because he has promised never to turn away from those who truly seek him.

SINGING IN TUNE

Urgent troubles bring about urgent prayer. David comes to God with no opening formalities. He just pours out his pressing need (vv. 1–2). Only trust enables that kind of confident prayer, trust that deepens with every new deliverance. David trusted, which is why he asks God to be for him in the present what he has proven to be in the past—a rock of refuge and a strong fortress (vv. 3–4). David not only trusted God; he also entrusted himself into God's care and refused to consider any form of false hope (vv. 5–6). When we trust God for deliverance, he makes us safe, and when we trust him to forgive, he covers us with grace (vv. 7–10). Trust doesn't earn us God's favor, but his favor does deepen our trust. Loved ones let us down, and some turn against us outright, but God will never let us down. God is unfailingly faithful (vv. 11–14). We can trust him utterly, because he determines our days. He decides what sorrows to allow and which ones to prevent. He controls both what we have and what we lack. He chooses our course for us (v. 15). David knows God—that he is good—and, for that reason, he can joyfully await deliverance. God will protect him and outwit his enemies (vv. 19–22), and as he waits, David encourages others in crisis to wait expectantly with him (vv. 23–24).

MUSICAL NOTES

God's Grace

David's deep love for the Lord and his trust were rooted in his experience with the Lord. Time and again God rescued him, but not because David was worthy—David knew he was not! The same is true for all God's people, including us. Each and every deliverance comes only through God's abundant grace. In this way, God teaches us to love him.

God's Attributes

- blessing
- delivering
- good
- guiding
- hearing
- overruling
- rescuing

SING THE SONG

Explain how 1 Peter 1:3–10 deepens your understanding of Psalm 31.

Psalm

⋙ 32 ⋘

Set Free and Forgiven

THEME

Confession of sin and repentance lead to restoration of joy.

HARMONY

Psalm 32 was composed by David as a song of thanksgiving for the forgiveness of his sin. Although the storyline of the psalm is personal, it was meant to be sung by any and all of God's people.

SINGING IN TUNE

A sinful habit can become so entwined with our identity or daily routine that cutting it off seems impossible. We don't know how we can live without it. So we make excuses and look for loopholes. We settle for minimizing it rather than killing it. That's where David's sin had taken him (vv. 3–4). Knowing that God is waiting with open arms to receive us, we can do what David did—stop excusing and start confessing. When we do, we will enjoy the freedom of broken shackles and the lightness of a clean conscience (vv. 5–6). Unrepentant sin darkens our understanding and skews our view of God; we cannot see him clearly when our backs are turned. But when we turn around and run toward him, his grace comes back in view (v. 7). Repentance restores us to God's paths, and it humbles our hearts to follow his ways. God is faithful to keep his covenant promise never to let us go, and for that reason, he doesn't leave us to ourselves. He is faithful to stop his straying people in their fleeing tracks (vv. 8–10).

David calls upon all God's people to find the joyful renewal that comes with repentance (v. 11).

MUSICAL NOTES

God's Grace

David confessed his sin and was restored to joy, but his confession wasn't the reason God forgave him. The sentence on all sin is death, and because God is just, all sin must be paid for. That's why prayers of confession simply aren't enough. Our guarantee of forgiveness comes only through faith in Jesus, the One who took on himself the death penalty we deserve. In him God hears our prayers, forgives all our sin, and freely restores us to the joy of his salvation.

God's Attributes

- faithful
- forgiving
- merciful

SING THE SONG

Note all the similarities you see between Psalm 21 and 1 John 1:5–10.

$\mathcal{P}salm$

~~~ 33 ~~~

The Unfailing Love of God

THEME

The Creator and sustainer of the universe can be trusted to care for his people and provide everything they need.

HARMONY

Psalm 33, a song of praise, lifts up God's greatness and celebrates the privileges that come to those who belong to him. Praise psalms were sung when Israel gathered for public worship.

SINGING IN TUNE

"Sing to him a new song" (v. 3)—God's people can sing anew, even with an old composition and well-worn lyrics. The song might be old, but the outpouring of God's love is new every day, and it is this of which God's people sing. God's righteous rule determines the daily course of the world he created, from the waves of the sea to the kings of nations (vv. 5–10), and in it all, he works to the benefit of his own people (vv. 11–12). God not only knows everything that will happen—he has determined it, to the fashioning of every human heart (vv. 13–15). For that reason, looking elsewhere for security is futile (vv. 16–17). God takes special note of those who trust him, and he proves worthy of their trust as he rescues them from trouble and provides for their needs (vv. 18–19). Deliverance may seem far off and provision out of reach, but joy and hope abide in those who know him, because he proves again and again that he never fails his people (vv. 20–22).

MUSICAL NOTES

God's Grace

The earth is indeed "full of the steadfast love of the LORD" (v. 5), evidenced most fully in the sending of his Son. "For God so loved the world, that he gave his only Son, that whoever believes in him should not perish but have eternal life. For God did not send his Son into the world to condemn the world, but in order that the world might be saved through him" (John 3:16–17).

God's Attributes

- delivering
- directing
- faithful
- guiding
- loving
- overruling
- trustworthy

SING THE SONG

Build on what you learn about God in Psalm 30 by meditating on Ephesians 1:3–12.

Psalm

~*~ 34 ~*~

Taste and See

THEME

Those who trust in God are never disappointed.

HARMONY

Psalms sung in celebration of God and his covenant faithfulness are called "praise psalms" and "thanksgiving psalms." Psalm 34 was composed by David to express thanks to God for rescuing him from a dangerous situation, which is recounted in 1 Samuel 21:10–22:1.

SINGING IN TUNE

David had acquired a reputation for courage in dangerous situations, but he attributes his rescue to the delivering hand of the Lord (vv. 1–7). Threats and danger were regular occurrences in David's life, yet in each one he sought the Lord, prayed for rescue, and experienced deliverance, and he invites all God's people to get a taste of this divine goodness (v. 8). When they do, they will discover that God is all he has promised to be. Those who trust God and walk in his ways are divinely supplied with everything they need to keep on trusting and walking (vv. 9–10). David adds some practical wisdom to his song: people who enjoy God's blessings are those who guard their lives from sin, pursue paths of righteousness, and nourish their relationships (vv. 11–17). David notes that God is especially tender toward the brokenhearted and comes to their aid. God in his wisdom allows grief and pain, but he also comforts our sorrows and does something about them (vv. 18–19). His people are ever safe in his care (vv. 20–22).

MUSICAL NOTES

God's Grace

Sometimes we are tempted to doubt; we believe that David was taking poetic license when he describes the extent of God's care for us. But Jesus's years on earth proved that every word of David's song is true. Jesus loved to heal the sick and comfort the sorrowful. He still does. He redeems the broken places in our lives, restoring and healing, and one day he will take us to be with him, and sorrow will be no more.

God's Attributes

- comforting
- delighting
- delivering
- good
- healing
- providing
- redeeming

SING THE SONG

Explain how Romans 12:1–2 and 1 Peter 2:1–3; 5:6–10 can help you apply Psalm 34.

Psalm

~~~ 35 ~~~

A Prayer for Justice

THEME

Prayers for the downfall of the wicked uphold God's righteousness.

HARMONY

Psalm 35 is a song of prayer against evil. Psalms with this theme are called "imprecatory psalms," and they serve a dual purpose: to uphold God's righteousness and to annihilate evil. Since the song was sung in public, those committing the evil might hear it, be warned, and turn to God themselves. David composed Psalm 35.

SINGING IN TUNE

David's enemies are more than he can handle; he is in desperate need of God's help to battle not only the enemy but also the temptation to doubt (vv. 1–3). We might be inclined to skip over much of his song—the prayer for the destruction of his enemies—because it just seems to go against everything we know about godly character. But since the Bible is where we find these hard words, it can't be wrong. David's prayer is not only right; it is also realistic, because in order for God to protect his people, those who harm them must be stopped. Underlying David's prayer was God's long-range plan to enfold enemy outsiders into the community of his people, and in David's day, military victory was the way in which God accomplished that purpose. Ultimately, God desires all his enemies to be conquered by conversion.[2] David ends on a note of praise, rejoicing that

God delights in the welfare of his people, which God himself ensures, and in that God is glorified (vv. 27–28).

MUSICAL NOTES

God's Grace

People in high positions, such as King David, are not the only ones who deal with enemy threats on a regular basis. We all do. Our enemies are likely not covert military operatives (although for some of us, they might be). More often than not, the threats we endure are more spiritual and emotional than physical. But the truth is, our greatest enemies—sin and Satan—threaten our complete destruction, and it's with those enemies in mind that we can sing this song with passion. At the cross, Jesus defeated sin and Satan so that those who put their trust in him will surely be delivered. So we stay in the fight, confident that he has already provided all we need for victory. "If God is for us, who can be against us?" (Rom. 8:31).

God's Attributes

- conquering
- protecting
- saving
- vindicating

SING THE SONG

Ponder Romans 12:17–21.

Psalm

❧ 36 ❧

Love—Rejected or Embraced

THEME

Hardened hearts grow increasingly dark, but those who trust in the Lord rejoice in his love.

HARMONY

David composed Psalm 36 to expose the contrast between the hard heart of unbelievers and the loving heart of God.

SINGING IN TUNE

Sin is the driving force of those who reject God and the primary motivator for all they think and do. They warp their hearts by making much of themselves and little of God (vv. 1–2), and warped hearts make warped choices that lead to ruin (vv. 3–4). The wicked are callous, self-involved, and foolish. They are blind to the truth of God, whose love and faithfulness are boundless (vv. 5–6). Unlike the wicked, the godly seek life in God and his ways, and there they find complete satisfaction (vv. 7–9). Given the prevalence of evil and wicked people, David prays for continual evidences of God's love, especially in keeping evil at bay and eventually eradicating it altogether (vv. 10–12).

MUSICAL NOTES

God's Grace

David's description of the wicked applies to each of us unless God intervenes to save us. As he shows in his song, evil deeds originate from evil hearts, and no one can change her own heart. "But God, being rich in mercy, because of the great love with which he loved us, even when we were dead in our trespasses, made us alive together with Christ . . . so that in the coming ages he might show the immeasurable riches of his grace in kindness toward us in Christ Jesus. For by grace you have been saved through faith. And this is not your own doing; it is the gift of God" (Eph. 2:4–8).

God's Attributes

- faithful
- judging
- loving
- righteous
- saving
- supplying

SING THE SONG

Follow your reflection on Psalm 36 by thinking through Romans 1:18–25; 5:6–11.

Psalm

❧ 37 ❧

Fulfilled in God

THEME

Trusting in God and walking in his ways is the only path to fulfillment.

HARMONY

Psalm 37 has lots of similarity to the teaching and wording of the Bible's Wisdom Literature, primarily the book of Proverbs. The psalms that mirror the Bible's wisdom teaching are called "wisdom psalms."

SINGING IN TUNE

We look around at what others have and what we seem to lack, and it stirs up wanting, which in turn leads to discontentment if we can't lay hold of it. But much of what stirs this envy is only an illusion, for those who have everything by this world's standards really have nothing if they live apart from the Lord (vv. 1–2). The key to life is to take our eyes off the world and its short-lived pleasures and put our trust in God and his ways (v. 3). In him we find the fulfillment we've always hungered for. Those who walk in his ways are shaped in those ways, and the result is contentment, peace, and personal prosperity (vv. 4–11). Walking with God also reshapes our perspective on the world and sin. No longer do we fret over what others have or fear what they might take from us, because we see their desperate greed, the futility of their plans, and how they blight the lives of their own children (vv. 12–17, 20–21, 32–33). God sees all they do, and he will bring their evil to an end (vv. 35–36, 38). Conversely, those who walk with God in humble trust receive guidance, provision, justice, and joy for all time in God's presence (vv. 33–34, 37, 39–40).

MUSICAL NOTES

God's Grace

"The salvation of the righteous is from the LORD," sings David (v. 39). When we look to God for life, all the promises we find in this song come to us, but not because we merit them. We cannot save ourselves or spiritually qualify by anything we say, think, or do. God himself saves us, uniting us to Jesus Christ by faith. In him we are transformed from the inside out to want what God wants for us and to walk in his ways and to receive everything God has promised to be and to do for those who trust him.

God's Attributes

- delivering
- fulfilling
- giving
- just
- prospering
- righteous
- saving
- trustworthy

SING THE SONG

Consider how 2 Peter 1:3–8 helps you apply Psalm 37.

Psalm

❧❧❧ 38 ❦❦❦

The Consequences of Sin

THEME

The painful consequences of sin awaken our need for God's mercy and desire for restoration.

HARMONY

Lament psalms sometimes include an acknowledgment of sin. Such is the case in Psalm 38. These songs of repentance, sometimes called "penitential psalms," were prayerfully sung by individuals, as is the case with David here, and other times by God's people as a whole. In either case, we find no anxious fear in these songs, because God is merciful and kind, and he responds to his people's confessions with love and deliverance.

SINGING IN TUNE

Sin never pays, because that's how God designed the world to work. And what a mercy it is! Sin's consequences prove that sin doesn't pay, and they drive us to look for life elsewhere—in God and his ways. That's where David finds himself as he writes. He is suffering for his sin, and he has brought on himself the painful hand of God's discipline (vv. 1–2). David's sin apparently has both physical and relational consequences (vv. 3, 5, 11), and somehow it has opened the door to enemy invasion (vv. 12, 16, 19–20). Sin weakens every aspect of our lives. The only remedy is complete honesty before the Lord, confessing the sin as David did (v. 18). Then, even in the midst of his suffering, a note of hope shines through—God's mercy. David knows his God and that he can cry out for relief, even asking God to shorten the duration of his difficulties (vv. 21–22). Here he shows us that when sin's consequences befall us, we don't have to suffer in guilty silence; God invites our plea for merciful deliverance.

MUSICAL NOTES

God's Grace

The pain of regret is horrible, but this lowest of low points is the opening for restorative and freeing grace that we might never know otherwise. When the Lord hears our lament: "My iniquities have gone over my head; like a heavy burden, they are too heavy for me" (v. 4), he says in reply, "Come to me, all who labor and are heavy laden, and I will give you rest. Take my yoke upon you, and learn from me, for I am gentle and lowly in heart, and you will find rest for your souls. For my yoke is easy, and my burden is light" (Matt. 11:28–30). The consequences of sin are painful, but in Christ they are not permanent, and they are never punishment. Jesus bore that for us.

God's Attributes

- delivering
- fatherly
- merciful
- righteous

SING THE SONG

Explain how 1 Corinthians 11:27–32 and Hebrews 12:5–13 enrich your understanding of David's cries in Psalm 38.

Psalm

∞ 39 ∞

Humility in Hard Times

THEME

Turning to God in troubling circumstances changes our perspective and guides us out of trouble.

HARMONY

Psalm 39 is a lament. Prayerful songs such as this express all the varied emotions people experience during seasons of difficulty, and sometimes, as in Psalm 39, they include an acknowledgment of sin. Laments typically bend toward hope, even in the midst of trying times, teaching us that God welcomes boldness and honesty in our prayers.

SINGING IN TUNE

David doesn't tell us the backstory underlying his determination to keep his mouth shut, but clearly he was seriously provoked and troubled (v. 1). As he sought to hold back his words, his inner turmoil only grew stronger. Finally he does open his mouth, but rather than pouring out his indignation on those who are troubling him, he pours out his heart to God (vv. 2–3). We expect to hear angry words from David, but instead he asks God to remedy the situation, first by changing him. He prays for humility because it will give him an eternal perspective to better assess what's going on in his life. From that vantage point, he can see that the turmoil is relatively small in the overall scheme of life (vv. 4–6). His new-found humility enables him to wait for deliverance and to acknowledge his own sinful part in the problem (vv. 7–10). He seems to have brought at least some of the suffering on himself, and in that he recognizes the fatherly hand of God's discipline (vv. 11–12). He asks God to look away from his sin and to show him mercy (v. 13). Throughout his song, David emphasizes what he has done rather than what others have done to him, and from him we learn how to approach the Lord in our own challenges.

MUSICAL NOTES

God's Grace

David modeled for God's people how to process emotions and respond to evildoers, but despite his determination, his efforts were tainted by sin. Both his effort and his failure point to the need for One who would not fail—Jesus Christ. He guarded his mouth in the face of more persecution and torture than David ever experienced, and, unlike David, he had no sin of his own to contribute to his suffering. Our frail and faulty attempts to guard our words and humble our hearts are fully met in our Savior, "who, though he was in the form of God, did not count equality with God a thing to be grasped, but emptied himself. . . . And being found in human form, he humbled himself by becoming obedient to the point of death, even death on a cross" (Phil. 2:6–8). God has looked away from the failure of all who rest in Christ's perfection.

God's Attributes

- eternal
- fatherly
- merciful
- saving

SING THE SONG

Meditate on James 3:2–12 and 1 Peter 3:8–12.

$Psalm$

❧ 40 ❧

Wait for the Lord

THEME

As God delivers his people from trouble, they trust him more fully and long to tell others about his kindness.

HARMONY

Psalm 40 is both a song of thanksgiving and a lament. David thanks God for past blessings and prays for help in present trouble. His song also points to Jesus, especially verses 7–8, so for that reason, it is considered to be a "messianic psalm."

SINGING IN TUNE

God rewards patient trust, as David had discovered (v. 1). Time and again, God had delivered David from very real trouble, and because David was known throughout Israel, many witnessed these divine rescues and trusted themselves to God (vv. 2–3). Panic in times of crisis brings temptation to escape by any means possible, but waiting for the Lord to deliver is the only sure way forward (vv. 4–5). David obeyed God in performing the sacrifices that God required in those days, but God's pleasure wasn't in the sacrifices themselves. The heart of the worshiper is what God takes note of, and he finds pleasure in those who obey him joyfully (vv. 6–8). Even though David sought to please God, he sinned grievously at times, bringing troubles on himself and others along with the need for fresh mercies (vv. 11–15). Here, overwhelmed by sin, both his own and his enemies', David cries out for help, and because he knows God is faithful to his people, he confidently expects that rescue will soon come (v. 17).

MUSICAL NOTES

God's Grace

Even great kings like David waver in trust and obedience. Only King Jesus could rightfully claim, "Behold, I have come: in the scroll of the book it is written of me: I delight to do your will, O my God; your law is within my heart" (vv. 7–8). His obedience and never-wavering delight in God's will cover the fickle instability of his people.

God's Attributes

- faithful
- rescuing
- thoughtful
- trustworthy

SING THE SONG

Explain what Hebrews 10:4–10 adds to your understanding of Christ as he is revealed in Psalm 40.

Psalm

~~~ 41 ~~~

In Need of Healing

THEME

God hears the prayers of his suffering people and relieves those who
trust in him.

HARMONY

Psalm 41 is a lament. Here, David is perplexed that despite his efforts
to live in God's ways, he has fallen under sin and suffering. Even so, like
other laments, David's song reflects the confident hope of those who
trust their compassionate and faithful God. The psalms of lament teach
us that God welcomes boldness and honesty when we cry out to him, and
we need not fear that he won't hear, because he has promised never to
turn away from those who truly seek him.

SINGING IN TUNE

In the midst of great suffering, the psalmist finds hope in the fact that
God tangibly blesses those who care for the poor and needy (vv. 1–3). At
the same time, David knows those blessings aren't earned by good deeds.
His care for the poor is the fruit of his relationship with God, not the
source of it. In fact, he is in the midst of suffering as he writes his song,
some of which springs from his own sin (v. 4). On top of that, those who
hate him are making his suffering even worse. Perhaps most painful is
the betrayal of a close friend (vv. 5–9). So, suffering from sin and slander,

he cries out to God for rescue, and because God is faithful to his people, David is confident of deliverance (vv. 10–13).

MUSICAL NOTES
God's Grace

God shows compassion on us when we suffer, not because our faith is strong or because we do kind things for people, but because Jesus lived every painful thing we see in this psalm. He was hated by many and betrayed by friends. He even applied verse 8 to himself: "The Scripture will be fulfilled, 'He who ate my bread has lifted his heel against me'" (John 13:18). He knows what rejection feels like, so he knows exactly how to help us when we are rejected. Jesus's enemies got what they wished for—his death (v. 5). But he was raised up from death in order to raise us too. That's why no illness can destroy us, even if it takes away our life on this earth. In Jesus, we have been set in God's presence forever.

God's Attributes
- compassionate
- gracious
- healing
- protecting

SING THE SONG
Explain what Luke 4:16–21 adds to your understanding of Psalm 41.

The

PSALTER

Book 2

Psalm

⇢⇢ 42 ⇠⇠

Longing for the Lord

THEME

Times of loneliness and isolation create a hunger for God's presence and the fellowship of other believers.

HARMONY

Psalm 42 is a lament, and like other laments it serves as a prayerful out-pouring of raw emotion. Despite the painful circumstances that inspire the lament songs, a note of hope, rooted in faith, typically shines through. Psalm 42 is attributed to the Sons of Korah, who were appointed by King David to serve in music ministry.

SINGING IN TUNE

Memory mentors our moods, especially in trying times. While dealing with difficulty and cut off from the support of friends, the psalmist remembers happier days of fellowship with other believers when they would gather together for worship. Recalling his earlier happiness in-tensifies his present discouragement, making him long all the more for godly companionship and the very presence of God himself (vv. 3–4). Those memories darken his mood, but then he remembers something else—the character of God (v. 6), and he lays hold of those memories to scrape himself off the ground. He remembers God's love and how, even though he is cut off from fellow believers, God is still with him (v. 8). With a reminder of God's compassion firmly in view, he finds confidence to pour out his bewilderment in prayer, and afterward, his hope is restored (vv. 9–11).

MUSICAL NOTES

God's Grace

We are safe in Christ's keeping, but that doesn't mean life is trouble-free. God allows sorrow and lonely seasons into our lives as a way to deepen our desire for him as well as our capacity for true happiness. This is grace at work: "We rejoice in our sufferings, knowing that suffering produces endurance, and endurance produces character, and character produces hope, and hope does not put us to shame, because God's love has been poured into our hearts through the Holy Spirit who has been given to us" (Rom. 5:3–5).

God's Attributes
- comforting
- fulfilling
- hope-giving
- loving
- uplifting

SING THE SONG

Follow your reading of Psalm 42 by meditating on Matthew 5:6.

Psalm

❧ 43 ❧

A Cry for Hope

THEME

The world and its ways strive to keep us from God, but he is faithful to bring his people close to him and into the fellowship of other believers.

HARMONY

Psalm 43, composed by the Sons of Korah, is a lament. The psalms of lament teach us that God welcomes boldness and honesty in prayer, and we need not fear that he won't hear, because he has promised never to turn away from those who truly seek him. Psalms 42 and 43 go together.

SINGING IN TUNE

Asking God *why* isn't necessarily disrespectful. It all depends on the condition of the heart that's asking. The psalmist is perplexed that God seems silent and unwilling to come to his aid (v. 2). After all, his longing is for something good—to be back where God dwells with his people. Humility underlies his *why* question. He desires to understand more about God and his ways. God rejects the *why* of arrogant complaint, but he welcomes the *why* of humble seeking. The psalmist's humility is evident in his request for guidance. He wants to process his problem in the light of God's truth and be led by the light on God's path (v. 3).

MUSICAL NOTES

God's Grace

The psalmist feels rejected by God, but despite these feelings, he knows God hasn't abandoned him. He is hopeful that deliverance is coming. His confidence isn't based on the strength of his prayer or even on the rightness of his prayer request. His confidence is based on the truth that God is Savior (v. 5). God didn't reject the psalmist, nor does he reject us, because he allowed his Son to be rejected instead. On the cross Jesus asked the *why* question too: "My God, my God, why have you forsaken me?" (Matt. 27:46). The answer to his question is the source of our hope.

God's Attributes

- defending
- guiding
- joy-giving
- protecting
- saving

SING THE SONG

Record the similarities you observe between Psalm 43 and 2 Thessalonians 3:1–5.

Psalm

~ 44 ~

A Cry for Help

THEME

Deliverance from suffering is sometimes delayed, but God will always prove himself faithful.

HARMONY

Hidden in Psalm 44 is a glimpse of God's overarching plan of salvation. The experiences described by the composers, the Sons of Korah, point forward to what Christ would experience in order to save God's people.

SINGING IN TUNE

God's Word is one long story of God's redeeming his people from trouble (vv. 1–3). He keeps his promises time and again, and our faith and trust increase as a result. We come to know him as the God who delivers. But what happens when rescue is delayed? A crisis comes, and God seems distant and uncaring (vv. 9–16). In our search to understand, we begin to wonder what we might have done to bring about the problem. Are we cherishing some sin in our heart? The believers in Psalm 44 do this self-examination, and their conscience is clear (vv. 17–21), so they are utterly perplexed by God's seeming silence, and they pray for a sign of his favor and presence (vv. 23–25). A clear conscience is not the basis for their request, however. It's God's love they plead. His love for his people is their hope for deliverance (v. 26).

MUSICAL NOTES

God's Grace

With a conscience free from guilt, God's people recognized that they were suffering for the sake of God's glory: "For your sake we are killed all the day long; we are regarded as sheep to be slaughtered" (v. 22). But they were delivered from suffering, as are we, because Jesus was not. For our sakes "he was oppressed, and he was afflicted . . . like a lamb that is led to the slaughter" (Isa. 53:7–10). Our deliverance from every trouble comes through his suffering on our behalf.

God's Attributes

- delivering
- kingly
- protecting
- redeeming
- saving

SING THE SONG

Describe how 1 Peter 4:12–19 builds on your understanding of Psalm 44.

Psalm

❧ 45 ❧

A Love Song

THEME

God's people celebrate a royal wedding, addressing first the husband-to-be, the king, then the bride, and finally her bridal party.

HARMONY

God appointed a line of kings, beginning with David, to lead his people in his ways. And God promised that through this line would come his greatest blessings (see 2 Sam. 7:12–17). Sure enough, when the kings served faithfully, all the people were blessed. Psalm 45 is a song celebrating the king's marriage. Psalms that rejoice in the king are called "royal psalms."

SINGING IN TUNE

All weddings are happy occasions, yet the one celebrated here had special significance not only for the bride and groom but also for all the people in attendance. The singers delight in the king's wedding attire and sing of his strength (vv. 1–3), because he leads them all in paths of righteous blessing. God's blessing of the king was an indicator that he was keeping his promise to provide a strong, righteous ruler to protect them (vv. 4–6). That promise reached its fulfillment in the final King of Israel—Jesus. Hints of the King of kings are glimpsed all through this song (vv. 6–8, 16–17). The bride isn't forgotten here. She too is celebrated (vv. 13–14), and she is encouraged to make her new husband her first priority (vv. 10–11).

MUSICAL NOTES

God's Grace

The joy of God's people at this wedding is only a shadow of the joy that we will experience at the wedding supper of the Lamb, Jesus Christ (Rev. 19:9). That's because we aren't mere subjects of the King—we are his bride. Jesus is both King and husband of God's people forever, bringing together in one person all that is celebrated in Psalm 45. And the blessings of this marriage aren't just held in reserve for heaven; they are for today as well and readily available to those who give Christ their hearts and forsake competing loyalties (v. 10).

God's Attributes

- beautiful
- eternal
- kingly
- majestic
- protecting
- providing
- strong

SING THE SONG

Describe how Revelation 19:6–9 shows the fulfillment of Psalm 45.

Psalm

⤳ 46 ⤶

Mighty Fortress

THEME

When chaos abounds, from natural disasters to the wars of nations, there is no reason to fear, because God controls his creation and everyone in it.

HARMONY

The safe "city of God" (v. 4) is Zion, Jerusalem, which housed the temple, the special place where God revealed his presence, protection, and power to his people. This special gathering place was a shadow of a greater temple to come. It came in the form of a person, Jesus Christ, and all those united to him by faith become part of a spiritual temple, the church. The big picture of the temple in Scripture is God and man dwelling in close fellowship together.

SINGING IN TUNE

Watching the news grows more unsettling by the day. If it's not dire warnings about the effects of climate change, it's the latest horrific terrorist attack. We fear for the future, most especially that of our children. But there's no need for fear when God is where we flee for safety. No matter what goes on in the world around us, he controls all things and works through them on behalf of his people (vv. 1–7). If anxiety threatens, we need to quiet our panic and take a look at God's mighty acts. He who controls the rise and fall of people and nations can control the details of his loved ones and protect them every moment (vv. 8–10).

MUSICAL NOTES

God's Grace

The river in God's city (v. 4) is a picture of endless, life-sustaining, thirst-quenching provision. Earth and its treasures give no lasting satisfaction, nor can they calm our fears or fulfill our hopes. God is the only one who can supply such water, and living in his presence is how we drink it and find its full benefits. We don't need to go to Zion for that today; we go to Christ. And when we turn to him, we hear the words he told a social outcast: "Whoever drinks of the water that I will give him will never be thirsty again" (John 4:14).

God's Attributes

- ever-present
- helping
- protecting
- ruling
- thirst-quenching

SING THE SONG

Explain what John 7:37–39 adds to your understanding of God as he is shown in Psalm 46.

Psalm

❧ 47 ❧

King of Joy

THEME

God's people celebrate him as King of the whole world.

HARMONY

God appointed a line of kings, beginning with David, to lead his people in his ways, and through this line God promised to bring his greatest blessings (see 2 Sam. 7:12–17). When the kings served faithfully, all the people were blessed. But ultimately they all failed, and all God's people suffered for it. Even so, the psalms rejoice in the king because God keeps his promises, and therefore the ideal King would one day come. Psalms that rejoice in the king are called "royal psalms."

SINGING IN TUNE

God had brought his people into the Promised Land, displacing the nations who'd been living there (v. 3). Many in these nations were destroyed at the Lord's command but not because God was cold and unfeeling toward everyone outside Israel. The destruction on the Gentiles was indeed God's judgment for their sin, but that's the fate of every human being unless God intervenes to save. And that's exactly what he was working out in leading Israel to conquer the Gentiles. It was all part of his long-range plan to bring people from those nations—and every nation down through history—to himself so that they can live in his light and enjoy his blessings (vv. 8–9).

MUSICAL NOTES

God's Grace

When God gave the land of Canaan—the Promised Land—to his people, everything in it became their "heritage" (v. 4). This heritage, or inheritance, included way more than just acres of land. It included all the people from that land who would join with God's people as part of his worldwide family. That family has been expanding ever since. Today it includes everyone who puts faith in the Lord Jesus. Once this big family has been fully gathered in, the King will give them "an inheritance that is imperishable, undefiled, and unfading" (1 Pet. 1:3–4).

God's Attributes

- compassionate
- holy
- purposeful
- royal
- sovereign

SING THE SONG

Explain how Romans 15:8–13 fulfills Psalm 47.

Psalm

❧ 48 ☙

City of God

THEME

God protects and leads his people.

HARMONY

The theme of Psalm 48 is Zion, the special city where the temple was built. There God revealed his presence, protection, and love to his people. Psalm 48 was composed to celebrate God's powerful work on behalf of those who dwell within Zion's walls.

SINGING IN TUNE

Living in close fellowship with God leads to praise and joy (v. 1). In the psalmists' days, such fellowship was centered in a particular place—Zion, or Jerusalem. From inside the city God's people could see firsthand that he protects and defends his own (vv. 3–8) because he loves them (v. 9). God's people valued Jerusalem because God was there. They walked around the city and marveled at its structure (vv. 12–13). It wasn't the architecture that awed them but what it represented—the character of God. They could see that God's righteousness produces joyful freedom (vv. 10–11), and they enjoyed the safety his guidance brings (v. 14).

MUSICAL NOTES

God's Grace

Today we don't have to go to a particular place to know God. We experience all those same blessings—even more fully—in Christ Jesus. "For in him all the fullness of God was pleased to dwell, and through him to reconcile to himself all things, whether on earth or in heaven, making peace by the blood of his cross" (Col. 1:19–20).

God's Attributes
- defending
- guiding
- joy-producing
- loving
- protecting

SING THE SONG

Describe how Revelation 21:22–27 fulfills Psalm 48.

Psalm

～ 49 ～

Fear Not!

THEME

Those who trust in God and live by his ways are able to recognize the futility of seeking security in wealth or worldly success.

HARMONY

Psalm 49 has lots of similarity to the teaching and wording of the Bible's Wisdom Literature, primarily the book of Proverbs. The psalms that mirror this wisdom teaching are called "wisdom psalms."

SINGING IN TUNE

Money can buy a lot of things, but it cannot buy life. The psalmist calls all people to ponder this riddle with him and sing the way to a solution (vv. 1–4). The power that accompanies wealth is fleeting, so there is no need to fear the rich or work to be like them (vv. 5–6). At the end of this life, we leave this world as we came into it—with nothing in our hands (vv. 9, 17–19). But what's in our hearts lasts forever and determines our eternal destiny (vv. 10–14). The wise live with this long-range perspective, and because of that, they aren't snared by a craving to have the best and the most in order to be admired by people (v. 18). Those who seek life from the Lord avoid this path of "foolish confidence" (v. 13), and they find eternal blessing.

MUSICAL NOTES

God's Grace

"Truly no man can ransom another," the psalmist said, "or give to God the price of his life" (v. 7). Only God can pay that price, which he did. He ransomed his people not with money but with blood—the shed blood of his Son. By his Son he redeemed us for himself so that we can live in his love and enjoy his presence. By faith in him we need have no fear of the rich and powerful or strive to be like them. We can sing to our Savior instead. "Worthy are you . . . for you were slain, and by your blood you ransomed people for God from every tribe and language and people and nation . . . and they shall reign on the earth" (Rev. 5:9–10).

God's Attributes

- eternal
- loving
- redeeming
- righteous

SING THE SONG

Meditate on Proverbs 18:11; Ecclesiastes 5:10; 1 Timothy 6:9–10; and Hebrews 13:5.

Psalm

~~~ 50 ~~~

Pleasing God

THEME

God, the Creator and ruler of everything, needs nothing from us, but he wants our hearts.

HARMONY

Asaph, appointed by King David to serve in music ministry in the house of the Lord, composed Psalm 50 to describe the sort of worship that pleases God. In his song Asaph speaks the very words of God to the people, much like the prophets did. For that reason, Psalm 50 is viewed as a "divine oracle."

SINGING IN TUNE

God directs the universe from day to day, from the course of the sun across the sky to the scampering of a field mouse (vv. 1, 10–11). Everything in creation bears his stamp of ownership (v. 12). Asaph uses this truth to demonstrate the silliness of trying to win God's favor by sacrifice—no one can give God what he already owns (v. 13). God commanded his people to offer him sacrifices, but it wasn't the animals he wanted. He was after the heart of the worshiper (v. 14). Some go through the motions of a devout spiritual life when their hearts aren't actually involved. They love sin rather than God, and over time, their real heart is exposed by how they live (vv. 16–20). Love for God is evidenced in gratitude, not primarily in word but in deed. When we love him, we obey him with gratitude rather than grumbling, and we serve because of what we've been given rather than what we hope to get. Such love is the only kind that pleases him (vv. 22–23).

MUSICAL NOTES

God's Grace

It's easy to do things for God; it's much harder to give him our heart. In fact, real love for him—the kind that results in right living and true worship—is possible only because he loved us first. Israel failed to love him truly, to offer right sacrifices with the right heart, and so do we. But he always knew we'd fail. Het set a standard impossible for sinners to meet in order to meet it for us, which he did by offering the sacrifice of his Son. "We love because he first loved us" (1 John 4:19).

God's Attributes

- delivering
- holy
- mighty
- saving

SING THE SONG

Describe how Hebrews 10:1–18 reveals the heart of God shown in Psalm 50.

Psalm

᠅ 51 ᠅

What True Repentance Looks Like

THEME

Genuine repentance brings restoration and renewal.

HARMONY

Psalms that express confession of sin are called "penitential psalms." Sometimes they were sung in a personal way, as is the case with David in Psalm 51, and other times they were sung by God's people as a gathered whole. In either case, we find no anxious fear in these songs, because God is merciful and kind, and he responds to his people's confessions with love and deliverance. David's tragic fall into sin is recounted in 2 Samuel 11–12.

SINGING IN TUNE

King David abused his leadership when he committed adultery with the wife of one of his warriors, Uriah, and then had Uriah killed to cover up the adultery. Not until confronted by Nathan the prophet was David guilt-stricken. His approach to God shows the pattern of all true repentance. It begins with a request for mercy (v. 1) and cleansing from guilt (v. 2). True repentance doesn't sugarcoat sin or excuse it (v. 3). David is stricken by the harm his actions have brought on others, yet he realizes that he has grieved God most of all (v. 4). David also realizes that his sin goes much deeper than adultery and even murder; it's actually part of his very nature (v. 5). We are not sinners because we sin; we sin because we are sinners. After his full confession, David prays for restoration to joyful fellowship with God (vv. 8, 12). A hallmark of all true repentance is a desire for God himself more than a desire for relief from sin's consequences, yet God often works through sin's sad consequences to reshape our lives into something new and beautiful (v. 13).

MUSICAL NOTES

God's Grace

The consequences of sin can last a lifetime, but God restores us the moment we turn back to him wholeheartedly, as David did. "If we confess our sins, he is faithful and just to forgive us our sins and to cleanse us from all unrighteousness" (1 John 1:9). But our confessing isn't the reason God forgives; our confessions are simply the path back to enjoying him (vv. 10, 16–17). Christ has already paid for every sin we will ever commit.

God's Attributes
- cleansing
- loving
- merciful
- renewing

SING THE SONG

Describe how 1 John 1:5–10 builds on the view of God shown in Psalm 51.

Psalm

~~ 52 ~~

Safe in God's Care

THEME

Fear and panic are unnecessary because God controls everything and everyone, and he has promised to protect his people.

HARMONY

David composed Psalm 52 to express confidence in God's care and protection, no matter what threatens. The backstory of Psalm 52 is found in 1 Samuel 21–22, and although it pertains to a specific situation in David's life, the message of the psalm was for all God's people.

SINGING IN TUNE

Nothing rattles God's love for his people or distracts his attention from them (v. 1). Conversely, those who reject God are characterized by love for sin (v. 3). They stir up trouble, but ultimately they will not prevail. God himself will stop their wicked work and bring them to an end (v. 5). When that happens, God's people will laugh—not from callous cruelty but from joy that God keeps his promises (vv. 6–7). So even when evil rages all around us and threatens our lives and loved ones, we can continue to thrive because we are safe in God's love (v. 8), and in the company of God's people we can wait in confidence for God to act (v. 9).

MUSICAL NOTES

God's Grace

Personal difficulties and opposition from others can shake up our confidence in God. We question why he doesn't intervene, and we wonder if he can really be trusted. But the things we suffer are actually a sign of his favor, and we can be sure he is at work in them to increase our capacity for joy and hope (see Rom. 5:3–5).

God's Attributes

- defending
- just
- protecting
- righteous
- shielding

SING THE SONG

Consider how Philippians 1:27–30 helps you to apply Psalm 52.

Psalm

~53~

The Fate of Fools

THEME

People who reject God destroy their lives and harm others.

HARMONY

David composed Psalm 53 to lament the reality that people in general reject God and refuse to seek him. Psalm 53 shares a good bit of wording with Psalm 14, so these psalms were likely two versions of a single song.

SINGING IN TUNE

Fools reject God by claiming there is no God (v. 1), but in reality, they are simply denying what they know to be true. They duck the reality of God by reveling in sin and by seeking to destroy those who willingly believe (v. 4). Ultimately, suppressing the truth about God darkens the understanding (v. 2), corrupts the heart (v. 3), hardens the conscience (v. 4), and terrorizes the soul (v. 5). Those sad consequences occur when God finally rejects those who are unremittingly determined to reject him. Along the way, they do all they can to crush God's people, but they will not succeed (v. 6).

MUSICAL NOTES

God's Grace

No one—not a single one of us—pursues God unless God first works in our hearts. So even our seeking is his gift. We turn to him only because he draws us. And he does! "You are a chosen race, a royal priesthood, a holy nation, a people for his own possession, that you may proclaim the excellencies of him who called you out of darkness into his marvelous light" (1 Pet. 2:9).

God's Attributes

- all-knowing
- holy
- just
- righteous
- saving

SING THE SONG

Explain what Romans 1:18–25 adds to your understanding of both God and human beings.

$\mathcal{Psalm}$

❧❧ 54 ❧❧

Delivered from Every Trouble

THEME

The Lord protects and delivers those who turn to him in faith.

HARMONY

David composed Psalm 54 as a lament. Laments are prayerful songs that express the wide range of emotions that can accompany difficult circumstances. They also reveal hope and trust in the promise-keeping God. The psalms of lament teach us that God welcomes boldness and honesty when we cry out to him. We need not fear that he won't hear, because he has promised never to turn away from those who truly seek him. The events that underlie Psalm 54 are recounted in 1 Samuel 23:19.

SINGING IN TUNE

Underlying David's lament was betrayal, which always brings grief, and in David's case, the betrayal led to an increased threat to his very life. With all this weighing heavily on his heart, he turns directly to God for help (vv. 1–2), appealing to God's name—all that's wrapped up in God's character and promises. Sinful actions arise from wrong thinking, as was the case with David's betrayers: "They do not set God before themselves" (v. 3). What we set our hearts on always determines what we do. A heart set on God trusts him to help and rests in confident security (vv. 4–5). The natural response to betrayal is hurt and anger, but those fixed on God are able to let go of such anger and leave vindication in his hands (v. 7).

MUSICAL NOTES

God's Grace

Even when deliverance from difficulty seems distant, we can be confident, as David was, that it will surely come. God has promised to provide a way out of every trouble we face. Often his rescue is swift; sometimes it awaits the next life. In either case, in love he determines when, where, and how our rescue will come. And we can be sure it will, because he has already rescued us from our sin and anchored us in the safety of his Son.

God's Attributes

- delivering
- helping
- listening
- sustaining

SING THE SONG

Meditate on Romans 8:31–39.

Psalm

❧ 55 ❧

Betrayal

THEME

David pours out his anguish to God following betrayal by a close friend.

HARMONY

David composed Psalm 55 to express his anguish over betrayal by a close friend. Confidence in God underlies this song of lament, even in David's prayer for the destruction of evildoers. His request is driven not only by a desire for deliverance but also for the triumph of righteousness over evil. Such prayers are characteristic of "imprecatory psalms."

SINGING IN TUNE

David's song reminds us of the freedom we have to pour out our emotions to a listening God. That's what David does with his hurt. A close friend has turned against him, and David struggles with how to deal with it. David begins his prayer with a personal plea for mercy (v. 1); he is well aware that he isn't sinless, even though in this case he is the one wronged. The pain of his betrayal makes him restless (v. 2), and remembering the former friendship causes him anguish (vv. 4, 13–14). He wants nothing more than to escape the pain (vv. 6–8). His former friend continues to cause trouble, and David knows that only God can effectively intervene (vv. 9–15). God never tires of his people's cries, so

David prays relentlessly for relief, leaving the solution in God's hands (vv. 16–18, 22–23).

MUSICAL NOTES

God's Grace

God fully understands the pain of betrayal. One of Jesus's close companions, Judas, betrayed him, and later even Jesus's closest inner circle abandoned him when associating with him proved costly. Since he experienced this sort of pain, he knows exactly how to enter in and help us when we turn to him for comfort and vindication.

God's Attributes

- befriending
- comforting
- judging
- protecting
- rescuing
- sustaining

SING THE SONG

Explain what 2 Corinthians 1:8–11 adds to the picture of suffering in Psalm 55.

Psalm

❧ 56 ❧

If God Is for Us...

THEME

God is for his people, so they have no reason to fear when others rise up against them.

HARMONY

David composed Psalm 56 as a lament, but his song is laced with thanksgiving too. As in all his laments, overwhelming circumstances distress him, yet confident hope dominates. He shows through his song that God welcomes boldness and honesty when we cry out to him. The particular crisis David was facing is recounted in 1 Samuel 21:10–15.

SINGING IN TUNE

No matter where David turns, he can't find safety, and as the dangers increase, so does his fear. But he doesn't sink under it; instead, he puts his trust in God. Firmly anchored trust not only quells his fears; it also changes his perspective on his problems (vv. 3–4). His enemies continue to pursue him, but God sees and knows every harmful thought, word, and deed they do, and God will call them to account (vv. 5–9). Even before deliverance comes, David sings praises and prepares for thanksgiving. He trusts God's promise to free him from every hindrance to his walk of faith (vv. 12–13).

MUSICAL NOTES

God's Grace

David trusted God because he was fully convinced that no matter who turned against him, God was for him (v. 9). We have that same assurance in Jesus. "If God is for us, who can be against us?" asks the apostle Paul, and then he answers his own question: "He who did not spare his own Son but gave him up for us all, how will he not also with him graciously give us all things?" (Rom. 8:31–32). In Jesus, God is for us, and he alone determines our destiny and all the particulars along the way.

God's Attributes

- attentive
- gracious
- just
- protecting
- trustworthy

SING THE SONG

Explain how Romans 8:26–39 deepens your understanding of Psalm 56.

Psalm

❧ 57 ☙

The Blessing of Caves

THEME

Trust in God grows stronger when we are helpless.

HARMONY

David composed Psalm 57 as a lament. In these prayerful songs, pain and desperation overlap with confident hope. The psalms of lament reveal that God's people are invited to approach him with candor, and they can be confident that he hears and responds. The background for Psalm 57 is most likely 1 Samuel 22:1.

SINGING IN TUNE

With nowhere else to go, David flees from Saul and hides in a cave. At this low point in his life, David prays to see tangible evidence of God's gracious kindness (vv. 1–3). Humility underlies his plea—he acknowledges his desperate need of help. But because David trusts God, even the lonely, dark cave and the enemies breathing down his neck are not enough to discourage him (v. 7). So confident is David of deliverance that he makes plans for the future—in a time to come, David will tell others of God's rescuing love (v. 9). David's trust in God keeps him from becoming preoccupied with himself—a common temptation in hard times. Instead he is preoccupied with God so that twice in this song he prays that God will be magnified to the watching world (vv. 5, 11).

MUSICAL NOTES

God's Grace

David was a rising star in the political landscape of his day, but he placed no confidence in that. Instead he was grounded in the conviction that God's purposes for his life would be fulfilled (v. 2). That same confidence is ours in Christ Jesus. God has specific plans for each one of his people, and he is able to bring them about, from the present all the way through till the end of our life (Rom. 8:28–30). United to Christ, we, like David, have no need to fixate on ourselves—our problems and goals and desires. Instead, we can focus on God, because he has already determined our destiny, and it is good.

God's Attributes

- faithful
- glorious
- loving
- merciful
- sovereign

SING THE SONG

Describe what Ephesians 2:1–10, together with Psalm 57, adds to your understanding of God's ways with his people.

Psalm

❧ 58 ☙

Evil Judged

THEME

When unjust rulers come to power and the people they rule are made to suffer, God will judge them.

HARMONY

David composed Psalm 58 as a lament for the whole community to sing when they were suffering oppression by unjust leaders. He prays for vindication and for the destruction of evil people, but revenge is not his motive; his request was driven by a desire for deliverance and also for the triumph of righteousness over evil. For that reason, songs like Psalm 58 can lead us to pray not only for the end of evil but also for those in authority to promote God's righteous ways.

SINGING IN TUNE

When evil leaders rule, all of society suffers, and from David's song we see that God's people have a role in rebuking the evil they see (vv. 1–2), even if the hearts of those who promote wickedness are so hardened that they cannot hear (vv. 3–5). In time God will judge wicked authorities who refuse him and his righteous ways. He will strip away their power and destroy them. Knowing of God's coming judgment, David prays for God's will to be done (vv. 6–9) so that, in God's timing, the watching world will see that evil fails, righteousness is rewarded, and the Lord is God Almighty. A holy God must bring judgment, but his heart longs to save, not destroy. Therefore, even in judgment, there is hope that "mankind will say, 'Surely there is a reward for the righteous; surely there is a God who judges on earth'" (v. 11).

MUSICAL NOTES
God's Grace
God's grace equips us to see Psalm 58 as a celebration of righteousness and the end of the suffering that evil inflicts. Wickedness is rooted not in people's deeds but in their hearts. All of us, not just some, are born estranged from God (v. 3), dominated by sin in thought, word, and deed. Because of that, we cannot make ourselves righteous. Righteousness comes from another source, Jesus Christ. All who are united to him by faith are made righteous, and they have nothing to fear when the final day of judgment comes.

God's Attributes
- just
- righteous
- saving

SING THE SONG
Consider Romans 13:1–5 in light of Psalm 58. Explain why the passage in Romans adds to rather than contradicts the message of the psalm.

Psalm

❧ 59 ☙

A Path through Injustice

THEME

When the threat of evil wearies the soul, remembering God's love strengthens and provides hope to persevere.

HARMONY

Hunted and wearied, David composed Psalm 59 as a song of lament. He pours out in prayer the injustice he's suffering, and as he does, he prays not only for deliverance but also for the destruction of his enemies. This was no personal vendetta on David's part; his request was driven for the triumph of righteousness over evil. For that reason, songs like Psalm 59 show us how to pray when evil of any sort threatens us. The background for Psalm 59 is 1 Samuel 19:11–12.

SINGING IN TUNE

Saul's pursuit of David was relentless. He was determined to end David's life. Hunted and in hiding, David cries out to God for protection and an end to the ordeal. He knows he's not sinless, but in this case, he's suffering for no sin of his own (vv. 1–4). "Awake, come to meet me, and see!" he prays. He pleads for God to do something, as Saul and his men plot new strategies of attack every night (vv. 6–7). Although God has not yet acted, he sees and knows every injustice David has suffered (v. 8). David can't see God at work, but he vows to watch for him, trusting that God will get him out of his plight (vv. 9–10). He also prays for the downfall of the evildoers and for the failure of their plans in order "that they may know that God rules over Jacob" (v. 13). In conquering evil, God draws souls. So David waits. God has proven himself faithful in times past, and no doubt he will do so again because he loves his people (vv. 16–17).

MUSICAL NOTES

God's Grace

Suffering injustice for our faith is actually a privilege. As we wait in hope for deliverance, we are blessed with a grace-fueled strength we wouldn't know any other way. On top of that, we have an opportunity to reflect Christ in how we handle our suffering, enabling others to see and marvel and ask us to give the reason for our hope. "Now who is there to harm you if you are zealous for what is good? But even if you should suffer for righteousness' sake, you will be blessed. Have no fear of them, nor be troubled" (1 Pet. 3:13–14).

God's Attributes

- defending
- delivering
- loving
- protecting
- strong

SING THE SONG

Describe how 2 Corinthians 12:7–10 helps you to apply Psalm 59.

Psalm

ᵈ⅓⁾ 60 ᵈ⅙⁾

God's Plans Will Prevail

THEME

Battling sin and evil can be disheartening, but victory is sure because God has decreed it.

HARMONY

David composed Psalm 60 as a lament for the whole believing community to sing. Laments express perplexity, anguish, and pleas for mercy in the midst of painful circumstances, yet they also reflect the confident hope of those who trust their compassionate and faithful God. The background for Psalm 60 is likely 2 Samuel 8:1–14.

SINGING IN TUNE

Long before Israel was a world superpower, God instructed the people to go into the land of Canaan and possess it. His intentions were not solely to bless Israel; by sending in his people, God intended to bring many from those regions into his holy family. Israel succeeded by God's enabling, which is how they became so powerful. Nevertheless, native idol worshipers persisted in certain areas, so the work of conquering was not yet complete. The task was daunting, and at times unsuccessful, and David pours out his frustration, even questioning God and his ways (vv. 1–3, 9–10). From David we see "that a believer does not have to have his thoughts straight before he prays. When he turns to the Lord, the Lord will order his thoughts and comfort his heart."[3] Getting into God's presence restores right thinking, which happened to David. His confidence in victory is renewed as he remembers that God's good purposes for his people will prevail (vv. 6–8, 12).

MUSICAL NOTES

God's Grace

David reminds God's people of the "banner" to which they could flee for safety when the battle rages (v. 4). We too have a banner—Jesus Christ. He is our safety, our only protection against the world, the flesh, and the Devil. In him, under this banner, we can continue what Israel began so long ago—bringing God's truth to those who don't yet know him as we do. Military conquest is no longer the way; we conquer with the gospel.

God's Attributes

- conquering
- gracious
- purposeful

SING THE SONG

Explain how Matthew 28:18–20 reveals the progress of God's redeeming purposes since the writing of Psalm 60.

Psalm

~~ 61 ~~

Safe in Our King

THEME

When overwhelmed by difficulty, God's people can appeal to him for relief.

HARMONY

Psalm 61 is a prayerful song concerning the well-being of the king—not just David but the whole line of kings to come after him. God's people sang this song with great feeling, knowing that their welfare hinged on God blessing the king. Psalm 61 and other psalms like it were included in the Psalter as a way to seek God's purposes in the lives of all God's people.

SINGING IN TUNE

Trouble is unavoidable, which is why David sets a pattern for prayer when it comes. We are invited to cry out to God, even when our faith is weak and doubts tempt (vv. 1–2). At such times, deliverance is surely needed, but more vital still is God's comforting, strengthening presence (vv. 3–4). David's focus shifts as he prays specifically for God's protective blessing to cover the king, because God's blessings of protection and provision came to everyone through the king (vv. 6–8).

MUSICAL NOTES

God's Grace

David's prayer for an eternally reigning king wasn't answered in his lifetime. He died, as did the kings who came after him. Not for a thousand more years would the answer come. It came in Jesus, David's descendant, the King of kings, who sits enthroned at God's right hand. Through him comes the fullness of all God's blessings.

God's Attributes

- attentive
- faithful
- listening
- loving
- powerful

SING THE SONG

The well-being of God's people has always been tied to a God-appointed king. Now that the King of kings is reigning, we are secure forever, and our prayers are different. From 1 Timothy 2:1–6, explain what has changed.

Psalm

⇜ 62 ⇝

Wait for the Lord

THEME

When oppressed by powerful people, we can turn to God for help and rely on God for deliverance.

HARMONY

David composed Psalm 62 to express confidence in God's care and protection, no matter what threatens. For that reason, such songs are called "confidence psalms."

SINGING IN TUNE

God always hears the prayers of his people, and he can be trusted to answer in his perfect way and time. We have no need to latch on to worldly ways or to seek security in material blessings or powerful people (vv. 9–10). God alone can provide what we truly need, and we will never regret waiting for his provision (vv. 1–2, 8). God's provision is always personal—*my* rock, *my* salvation, *my* fortress (vv. 2, 6–7). When our cry for help seems to go unanswered, the only safe thing to do is wait (vv. 1, 5). But waiting on God is no nail-biting exercise in self-management; it involves active trust, reminding ourselves of all he has promised to be for his people.

MUSICAL NOTES

God's Grace

Godly confidence is rooted not only in what God *does* for us but in who he *is* for us. Trusting him means knowing we can be real with him, that we can tell him exactly how we feel and what we hope for. Such honesty, that unself-conscious realness, is the hallmark of any healthy relationship, including our relationship with God, and we've been brought into it through Jesus Christ, "in whom we have boldness and access with confidence through our faith in him" (Eph. 3:12).

God's Attributes

- listening
- protecting
- providing
- saving
- trustworthy

SING THE SONG

Meditate on Romans 8:26–27 and Hebrews 4:14–16.

Psalm

❧ 63 ☙

Longing for God

THEME

Prolonged difficulties produce an intense yearning for God.

HARMONY

David composed Psalm 63 to express confidence in God's care and protection, no matter what troubles press in. The song reflects David's struggle as he hides from enemies in the wilderness, but its message is for all God's people.

SINGING IN TUNE

Trying times deepen our longing for God. Often it takes a trial to expose the inadequacy of our self-made coping strategies and bring us to the end of ourselves. At such times we see all God is for us. Despite his many skills and proven strength, David had to run and hide in order to save his life on more than one occasion. Here in the desert wilderness, his longing for the Lord intensifies just as his body longs for relief from the harsh conditions of the desert (vv. 1–2). He has known that the Lord alone can satisfy (v. 5), and because of that, even though he is not yet out of trouble, his heart can offer praise (v. 3). God's hand upholds him even in the wilderness (v. 8), and he is able to wait for God with confidence that his enemies shall not have their way with him (vv. 9–11).

MUSICAL NOTES

God's Grace

The psalmist likens his enjoyment of God to feasting at a lavish meal, which is how God wants us to know him. The gospel is how we partake. We find hints of this in the call to Lady Wisdom's feast (Prov. 9:1–6). It was foretold through the prophet who spoke of water for the thirsty and free wine and milk to those who respond (Isa. 55:1). Most fully, we find it on the lips of Jesus himself, who promised living water and the bread of life to those who come to him (John 4:13–14; 6:35). One day, all who do will sit down at a feast that never ends (Rev. 19:9).

God's Attributes

- just
- loving
- satisfying
- upholding

SING THE SONG

Meditate on Philippians 3:1–16.

Psalm

❧ 64 ☙

The Terrifying Tongue

THEME

The schemes of the wicked will not prevail, because God protects his people.

HARMONY

David composed Psalm 64 to lament the oppressive persecution God's people suffer at the hands of evildoers. Similar to other laments, this song expresses confidence in the inevitable downfall of the wicked, a confidence rooted in the promises and character of God.

SINGING IN TUNE

The threat aimed at David isn't military weaponry but the tongue of his enemies. He has become aware of secret plots hatched by "bitter words" (vv. 2–3, 5), so he prays for protection (v. 1). Sin always comes back to bite the sinner, proving in the end that God's righteous ways prevail. In this case, those who use their words to plot evil will in turn be destroyed by those very schemes (v. 8). When God brings wicked words to nothing, God-glorifying words will be proclaimed (v. 9). God always prevails, and for that reason, even before deliverance comes, his people can rejoice in confident security (v. 10).

MUSICAL NOTES

God's Grace

David knew, and we know, the power of words. Jesus said that "out of the abundance of the heart the mouth speaks" and that our words will either justify or condemn us (Matt. 12:34, 37). In his thirty-three years on earth, Jesus's words were always loving, righteous, and God glorifying. He always knew the best thing to say and when to say it. No one else has ever done that, which is why we need a refuge, not only from the hurtful words of others but from the sinful words that come from our own lips. We find it in Jesus, because every righteous word he spoke covers the tainted tongue of all who hide in him.

God's Attributes

- just
- protecting
- purifying
- righteous

SING THE SONG

Meditate on Proverbs 18:7 and James 3:1–12.

Psalm

~~ 65 ~~

Irresistibly Drawn

THEME

God is worthy of praise for prospering the world he made and most especially his own people.

HARMONY

Many of the psalms were sung in celebration of God's greatness and the privileges that come to those who belong to him. These songs, called "praise psalms" and "thanksgiving psalms," were sung when Israel gathered for public worship. Psalm 65 was composed by David to celebrate a fruitful harvest. Jerusalem, or Zion (v. 1), was the special city of God's people, and there they gathered for worship.

SINGING IN TUNE

God is owed the praise of his people, David declares, so the people break out in song. God is praised for drawing them to enjoy his presence and for providing the means—atonement for sin and the gift of prayer—by which they can continuously experience the blessings of his fellowship (vv. 1–4). Everything God does and every answer to prayer spring from God's righteousness, which is why it is possible to have hope no matter what befalls us (v. 5). This is the God who rules the skies and the seas, and his work in creation points to his power (vv. 6–8) and to his good intentions to bless his people (vv. 9–13).

MUSICAL NOTES

God's Grace

Nothing is more satisfying than fellowship with God, most especially in the company of other believers. But left to ourselves, we would never choose the satisfying Lord; the perversity of our sin nature leads us to choose sinfully destructive paths instead. So God has done the choosing, irresistibly drawing particular people to experience his blessings, most especially freedom from the bondage and guilt of sin, through the atoning sacrifice of his Son on the cross. In Christ Jesus we are his precious children.

God's Attributes

- generous
- gracious
- kind
- powerful
- providing

SING THE SONG

Explain what John 6:44–51 adds to the revelation of God provided in Psalm 65.

Psalm

⤟ 66 ⤝

God's Wondrous Works

THEME

God works powerfully in all of creation to reveal his glory and bless his people, and those who know him can't help but sing his praise.

HARMONY

Psalm 66 is a praise song that was intended for all God's people to sing when they gathered together for worship. Like other songs of praise, Psalm 66 includes an invitation to outsiders to turn to God and worship him too.

SINGING IN TUNE

The psalmist invites the world to take note of God's deeds and give him praise (vv. 1–4), and then he directs his invitation specifically to the community of God's people, focusing their attention on God's work for them in times past. The Lord delivered them from slavery in Egypt, and he brought them across the Jordan River into the Promised Land (vv. 5–7). There is also a list of all that God does for his people on a daily basis. He preserves their lives and keeps them together as members of his own family (vv. 8–9), and he does this by disciplining them for disobedience and by testing their faith (vv. 10–12). After this, the psalmist gets personal, offering his own praise to God for answered prayer and reaffirming his desire to follow God's ways (vv. 13–15). The psalmist recounts his experience—how he poured out his longing to God while giving God praise, and God answered him (vv. 16–20). His testimony of the Lord's work is intended to encourage everyone to seek God and praise him too.

MUSICAL NOTES

God's Grace

God hears and answers our prayers, but if we cherish some sin in our lives, a prayer barrier is erected (vv. 18–19). It's not as though sin actually hinders God from hearing; it's that he won't be used, which is exactly what we do when we ask him to bless us while refusing to part with our sin. Yet God doesn't require sinlessness as the price for listening; if that were the case, we'd be without hope. We sin daily in word, thought, and deed. It's our heart God wants. God's ears stay wide open despite our repeated falls into sin, even the same old ones, when our lives are anchored in the sinlessness of Jesus.

God's Attributes

- almighty
- listening
- loving
- preserving
- providing

SING THE SONG

Consider how to apply Psalm 66 as you consider 1 Thessalonians 5:16–22 and 1 John 1:5–10.

Psalm

❦ 67 ❦

To Know God Is to Praise Him

THEME

A day will come when people from every nation on earth will know God and join together in worshipful praise.

HARMONY

Psalm 67 is a thanksgiving psalm that includes a prayer for God's blessing. The psalmist's request for the shining of God's face (v. 1) comes from Numbers 6:24–26, which is called the "priestly blessing."

SINGING IN TUNE

God's people celebrate the privileges of belonging to God, and they ask God to continue those privileges—grace, blessings, and the light of God's presence—so that those who don't know God will be drawn to him (vv. 1–3). The song then looks forward to a time when outsiders, those not of Israel, will be brought inside and become part of God's people, receiving his blessings and singing his praise (vv. 4–7).

MUSICAL NOTES

God's Grace

When the psalmist praises God for his guidance (v. 4), he has in mind specifically how God works to bring about faith in unbelievers, thereby enabling them to experience God's favor and blessings. God doesn't leave people to find him on their own; he goes after those he has marked out to belong to his family, and he brings them in.

God's Attributes

- giving
- gracious
- guiding
- providing
- saving

SING THE SONG

Consider how Romans 8:28–30 shows the fulfillment of Psalm 67.

Psalm

~~~ 68 ~~~

The Lord Triumphant

THEME

God showers kindness on his people and blesses them in every way, but those who reject him suffer loss and destruction.

HARMONY

Psalm 68 is a praise song that includes prayer for the defeat of those who oppose God, but the underlying hope is that their defeat will result in their conversion. Praise is given because "Sinai is now in the sanctuary" (v. 17), which is a reference to the ark of the covenant. The ark was a wooden chest specially made to hold the stone tablets on which were inscribed the Ten Commandments. These tablets represented the covenant God had made with all his people long ago through Moses on Mount Sinai.

SINGING IN TUNE

Belonging to God brings joy not only because of his saving work in the past but also because of his daily care in the present (vv. 19–20). God had led his people through the wilderness and into the Promised Land, enabling them to settle in and enjoy its lushness (vv. 4, 7–12). Afterward, God's people enjoyed even greater blessing because God dwelt in their midst in the sanctuary of Zion, his temple, where the ark of the covenant had come to rest (vv. 15–18), and from there he empowered his people to live for him (v. 35). Trials and troubles surely come, but God's people are characterized by joy because God provides for their every need. The Lord of reversals delights to turn tragedies into triumphs, especially for the weak and needy. He defends those who cannot defend themselves and meets their need for protection, provision, and fellowship (vv. 5–6). God's powerful work on their behalf in the past and his abundant provision in the present can serve as a witness and a warning to those who reject God (vv. 1–3, 21–23, 30). God's power and majesty ensure that he will always triumph over evil (v. 34), so only those who submit to his sovereign authority find life and blessing.

MUSICAL NOTES

God's Grace

God has a special tenderness for the poor and the outcast, and he is zealous to provide for their needs. He most often does so through the generosity of his people, who are commanded to care for the poor in practical ways. God's love for the weak is evidenced in his plans to use them to advance the gospel. In this way, the God of reversals actually provides for the strong through the weak. "God chose what is low and despised in the world, even things that are not, to bring to nothing things that are, so that no human being might boast in the presence of God" (1 Cor. 1:28–29).

God's Attributes

- defending
- fathering
- giving
- powerful
- protecting
- providing

SING THE SONG

Explain what 1 Corinthians 1:18–31 adds to your understanding of Psalm 68.

Psalm

❧ 69 ❧

Suffering Redeemed

THEME

God rescues those who suffer when they appeal to him for deliverance.

HARMONY

David composed Psalm 69 as a lament. It has special appeal to those who are suffering as the result of sin. Laments express perplexity, anguish, and even discouragement, yet they also reflect the confident hope of those who trust their compassionate and faithful God. The psalms of lament teach us that God welcomes boldness and honesty when we cry out to him, and we need not fear that he won't hear, because he has promised never to turn away from those who truly seek him.

SINGING IN TUNE

David is drowning in his troubles, and discouragement is taking hold. His enemies are stronger than he is, and although his own sin has played a part in his problems, the attack against him isn't warranted (vv. 1–6). In fact, his alignment with the Lord has contributed to the attack, and his suffering is pervading his entire life and relationships (vv. 7–9). David pours out the pain of his rejection and cries out for relief, asking God to judge his enemies and put a stop to their evil plans (vv. 10–29). Because he knows God's character, he is confident of deliverance and of being restored to his former well-being. God will not allow evil to have the last word. David hopes that those who sing his song will follow his lead, humbling themselves in repentance and experiencing restoration to the merciful God (vv. 30–36).

MUSICAL NOTES

God's Grace

Years later, Jesus echoed David's cries when he experienced persecution and was abandoned by those he loved. The difference is that Jesus's suffering was due not to his own sin but to ours. He bore the suffering we deserve so that we can enjoy the blessings he deserves. "For our sake he made him to be sin who knew no sin, so that in him we might become the righteousness of God" (2 Cor. 5:21). In Jesus's suffering, God delivers us from ours and leads us out into joyful praise.

God's Attributes

- delivering
- merciful
- redeeming

SING THE SONG

Meditate on Matthew 11:28–30; Luke 23:32–38; John 2:13–17; 15:23–25; and Romans 11:7–10; 15:1–4.

Psalm

❧ 70 ❧

An Urgent Prayer

THEME

God welcomes his people's cries for speedy deliverance.

HARMONY

David composed Psalm 70 as a lament. Psalm 70 was intended for singing during the "memorial offering," which the priests performed by burning some of the grain offering on the altar (see Lev. 2:2). It was a way of asking the Lord to remember them with blessing.

SINGING IN TUNE

Desperate circumstances call for desperate measures. That was the case with David, who in his song pleads with God to come quickly and help him (vv. 1, 5). His enemies are closing in, and they hatefully desire to see him suffer (vv. 2–3). David is confident that his prayer will be answered because he knows that thwarting evil is in keeping with God's will. If deliverance comes soon, all God's people will rejoice that good has triumphed over evil (v. 4). In the meantime, David is entirely dependent on God for deliverance; he can do nothing to help himself, which underlies the urgency in his song (v. 5).

MUSICAL NOTES

God's Grace

Poor and needy incline God's heart, not strong and self-sufficient. He pours out rescuing grace on those who trust him as their only hope. For that reason, God at times leads his people into desperate situations in which they can do nothing to help themselves. Only then will their hearts be sufficiently humbled to receive his help and give him the glory for it.

God's Attributes

- rescuing
- righteous
- saving
- timely

SING THE SONG

Note what 2 Corinthians 1:8–11 adds to Psalm 70 concerning prayer in times of trouble.

Psalm

❧ 71 ❧

Secure Forever

THEME

From birth until death, the Lord leads and protects his people.

HARMONY

David composed Psalm 71 as a lament while suffering unjust treatment. The suffering reflected in the lament psalms is often the result of oppression, persecution, or maliciousness aimed specifically at God's people.

SINGING IN TUNE

The Lord has kept David throughout his life, from the day of his birth (v. 6) up through his youth (vv. 5, 17), and David prays that God will continue to keep him close until the end (vv. 9, 18). Time and again, God has brought him safely through difficulty (vv. 6, 20), which strengthens David's confidence for deliverance in his current crisis (vv. 11–13). When rescue comes, he will find great joy in recounting God's saving work and singing God's praises publicly (vv. 6, 8, 14–15, 22–24).

MUSICAL NOTES

God's Grace

Trials and troubles plague us from the time we are born, and because of that, either we shake our fist in God's face, or we cling to him in trust. Were the decision left up to us, we'd turn away from God, but he preserves his people in their faith. He actually works in all our tribulations to that end. Therefore, those he has set apart for himself cannot walk away. "Now to him who is able to keep you from stumbling and to present you blameless before the presence of his glory with great joy, to the only God, our Savior, through Jesus Christ our Lord, be glory, majesty, dominion, and authority, before all time and now and forever. Amen" (Jude 24–25).

God's Attributes
- glorifying
- keeping
- protecting
- redeeming
- rescuing

SING THE SONG

Consider how Matthew 11:27–30 can serve as a companion passage to Psalm 71.

Psalm

~~~ 72 ~~~

A Good King

THEME

When a God-appointed king flourishes, so do the people he governs.

HARMONY

Solomon composed Psalm 72. Beginning with David, God appointed a line of kings to lead his people in his ways, and God promised that through this line would come his greatest blessings (see 2 Sam. 7:12–17). When David's reign ended, his son Solomon became king. When the kings served faithfully, all the people were blessed. That's why some of the psalms, like Psalm 72, are songs of rejoicing about the king. Even so, the ideal King was still a long way off, but he would one day come, and it's to him that these "royal psalms" ultimately point.

SINGING IN TUNE

From the beginning of his reign, Solomon knew that his success depended solely on God's blessing (see 2 Chron. 1:7–13), and here in Psalm 72 he outlines what true "success" looks like. The king must be characterized by God's justice and righteousness so that everyone from every class of society can prosper (vv. 1–4). The king must also be strong, not only morally but also militarily (vv. 5–11). The king's strength must be balanced by a tender heart for the poor and needy (vv. 12–14). Altogether, everything the king does should invoke the loyalty of his subjects so that they will uphold him as he leads (vv. 15–17). Such a king is a blessing not only to his people but to those of neighboring nations as well, who are welcome to come in and live under his dominion rather than fight against him. When this happens, outsiders are made insiders as they come to worship the Lord of the king, God himself (vv. 18–20).

MUSICAL NOTES

God's Grace

Solomon was for a time the greatest king the world had ever known, but he was unfaithful to God and pursued his personal passions instead. Nevertheless, Solomon's failure didn't ruin God's intentions to bless the whole earth through a king of Israel. Hundreds of years later, Jesus came to earth and fulfilled all the kingly responsibilities that the earlier kings did not. And unlike all the kings who came before him, Jesus's kingship didn't end with his death; he is King forever and ever. Jesus is the full and final answer to Solomon's prayer for a king who will bless all nations and fill the earth with God's glory.

God's Attributes

- compassionate
- delivering
- generous
- just
- kingly
- majestic
- strong

SING THE SONG

Explain how the answer to Solomon's prayer is seen in Revelation 19:11–16.

The

PSALTER

Book 3

Psalm

✧ 73 ✧

Where Contentment Is Found

THEME

God's people seem to have less and suffer more than those who reject God, so an eternal perspective is necessary for living contentedly in an unfair world.

HARMONY

Psalm 73, composed by Asaph, has lots of similarity to the teaching and wording of the Bible's Wisdom Literature, primarily the book of Proverbs. The psalms that mirror the wisdom teaching found in Scripture are called "wisdom psalms."

SINGING IN TUNE

Envy almost destroyed Asaph's faith because he envied unbelievers who indulge in life's pleasures with no restrictions (vv. 1–12). They do whatever they want and whatever feels good, and God seems to let them get away with it. Asaph was tempted to walk away from God, but he didn't. To the contrary, he turned *toward* God (vv. 16–17), and getting into the presence of God changed his thinking. His thoughts and desires were radically transformed as he focused on God in the company of God's people, and in the process he developed an eternal perspective. He realized that the wicked really have nothing, because everything they live for will sooner or later be destroyed—as will they themselves (vv. 16–19). Focusing on God also enabled Asaph to recognize his envy as sin (vv. 21–22), and in the process, his trust was renewed. So was his hope when he realized that in God, he already had everything that makes for lasting contentment (vv. 23–25).

MUSICAL NOTES

God's Grace

God is not insensitive to the cries and questions in our hearts. He never gets impatient, wishing we'd just get it together. That's why Asaph includes verse 26: "My flesh and my heart may fail, but God is the strength of my heart and my portion forever." God loves us despite our sinful dissatisfaction with his providences, and when we turn to him, our hearts will change, even if our circumstances don't, because he is faithful to his people.

God's Attributes

- faithful
- fulfilling
- good
- guiding
- strong
- sufficient

SING THE SONG

Describe how Philippians 4:10–13; 1 Timothy 6:6–8; and Hebrews 13:5 provide practical application for Psalm 73.

Psalm

~~ 74 ~~

Never Forsaken

THEME

God orchestrates even the bad that happens in the lives of his people and uses it redemptively.

HARMONY

Asaph composed Psalm 74 as a lament over the ruin of the sanctuary, the place where the believing community gathered to enjoy God's presence. The cries for deliverance in lament psalms are often reinforced with an appeal to God's reputation, as is the case in this song.

SINGING IN TUNE

When the consequences of sin come upon us, the suffering we experience makes sense, but many of our difficulties have no discernable reason. In either case, we can be tempted to think that God has abandoned us. That was the case in Psalm 74. Asaph leads the entire community in asking God why he has allowed evil to triumph over something good (vv. 1, 10–11). Without an answer, the people nevertheless ask God to come to their rescue, and they make their appeal based on all God has done for them in the past, giving them a special place for worship after leading them out of slavery in Egypt (vv. 2–3, 12–14). They are hungry to hear from God, but no word is forthcoming (v. 9). Nevertheless, while asking God to remember his promises to them, they remember him and who he has always been— powerful Creator and ruler of all (vv. 12–17).

MUSICAL NOTES

God's Grace

When crises come and we find ourselves in desperate need of deliverance, we too can cry out for answers and divine deliverance. As in Asaph's day, the only basis for our request is God's reputation, specifically that of his mercy. He has promised never to forsake us, even when we fail to honor him and stumble in sin. God's promise has been secured for all time through Jesus, whose perfect obedience fulfilled all God's requirements for us.

God's Attributes

- faithful
- just
- promise-keeping
- powerful
- righteous

SING THE SONG

Explain what Galatians 3:10–14 adds to the view of God provided in Psalm 74.

Psalm

～ 75 ～

Judgment Is Coming

THEME

God is the judge of the whole world.

HARMONY

Many of the psalms were sung in celebration of God's greatness and the privileges that come to those who belong to him. These songs, called "praise psalms" and "thanksgiving psalms," were sung when Israel gathered for public worship. Included in many of them, such as here in Psalm 75, is an implicit invitation to outsiders to avoid God's judgment by turning to worship him instead. Psalm 75 was composed by Asaph.

SINGING IN TUNE

God's righteous and just character is a joy for God's people but a dread to those who reject his authority. God has already determined the day of judgment, and on that day those who have arrogantly refused his lordship will be destroyed (vv. 2–5). The theme of "lifting up" is sprinkled through the song (vv. 4–7, 10), and it has to do with God's authority. He alone determines the destiny of each individual. God lifts some to great blessing. The ones he puts down are the arrogant who try to lift themselves up (v. 5), shunning God's authority over them. For this reason, God's people ultimately have nothing to fear from their persecutors, nor do they need to fear the final judgment (vv. 9–10).

MUSICAL NOTES

God's Grace

The "lifting up" of God's authority will reach its fulfillment on the last day, the day of final judgment, and what will happen on that day has already been determined, as Jesus declared: "Now is the judgment of this world; now will the ruler of this world be cast out. And I, when I am lifted up from the earth, will draw all people to myself" (John 12:31–32). Jesus was lifted up on the cross so that all who trust in his lifting, not their own, will enter eternal joy on the day of judgment.

God's Attributes

- just
- powerful
- righteous
- sovereign

SING THE SONG

Meditate on Romans 2:1–5; 9:18–24.

Psalm

❧ 76 ❧

Mercy or Judgment

THEME
God protects his people as they dwell together in his presence.

HARMONY
Psalm 76 was composed by Asaph to celebrate a tremendous victory over the enemies of God and his people. Asaph was appointed by King David to serve in music ministry at God's house.

SINGING IN TUNE
Jerusalem, the capital city of the nation of Israel, was named "Zion" when it became the special place God established for his people to fellowship together and worship. God's people cherished it for that reason and loved to sing about it, especially when God performed mighty works there that manifested his presence and power for all to see. Asaph recounts that haters of God and his people want nothing more than to destroy this special place, but they are no match for God (vv. 4–6). These foes would find life and blessing if they would set down their arms and submit to God while there is still time (vv. 10–12). Those who refuse and stubbornly continue to fight against him will sooner or later experience God's fearful judgment (vv. 7–9).

MUSICAL NOTES
God's Grace

"Surely the wrath of man shall praise you," sings Asaph (v. 10). What sounds like a contradiction to our ears is better heard as a paradox—a surprising, unexpected turn of events. When God demonstrates his power over evil and thwarts wicked schemes, many are humbled by his matchless power and so awed by his work that they stop fighting against him and turn to him instead. To all who come, "mercy triumphs over judgment" (James 2:13).

God's Attributes
- just
- majestic
- near
- powerful
- protecting

SING THE SONG

Describe what Romans 11:25–33 adds to what is revealed about God in Psalm 76.

Psalm

~~ 77 ~~

Remember the Lord

THEME

Remembering God's faithfulness in times past bolsters faith to trust in present suffering.

HARMONY

Asaph composed Psalm 77 as a lament. These prayerful songs express bewilderment and depression in the midst of overwhelming circumstances, yet hope for deliverance also comes into view when God's character and his past deliverances are called to mind.

SINGING IN TUNE

Long-endured suffering with no relief in sight can lead to both physical and spiritual depression. Even so, God is sensitive to the cries of his people as they call upon him during difficult days and sleepless nights (vv. 1–4). Depression and anxiety skew our perspective, but turning our thoughts to God always brings fresh clarity, as Asaph shows us. Fixing on God enables Asaph to "remember" (vv. 3, 6, 11), and as God's promises come freshly to mind, the psalmist takes himself in hand by asking a set of questions to which he already knows the answer (vv. 7–9). Of course the Lord has not forgotten to be gracious, nor has he cut off his compassion! Asaph then fuels his faith by calling to mind all God has done for his people in times past (v. 10), most especially in delivering them from slavery in Egypt and getting them through years in the wilderness (vv. 15–20).

MUSICAL NOTES

God's Grace

The worst of circumstances hide within them some of God's greatest blessings, because he is always at work for his people's good. The greater the difficulty, the more glory God receives when his behind-the-scenes work becomes evident, which is why, when the Egyptian army was closing in, God led Israel through the Red Sea rather than around it (v. 19). No matter the trouble, God is powerfully at work, causing all things to work together for good for those who love him (Rom. 8:28). No matter how bad things look, God is doing something for our good and his glory.

God's Attributes

- compassionate
- powerful
- purposeful

SING THE SONG

Describe how James 5:7–11 and 2 Peter 3:8–9 build on your understanding of Psalm 77.

Psalm

⤳ 78 ⟿

Our Faithful God

THEME

Proclaiming God's Word and works fosters faithfulness.

HARMONY

Psalm 78 is a "historical psalm" composed by Asaph. It was meant to serve as a history lesson to a younger generation to encourage them to walk faithfully with the Lord all their days.

SINGING IN TUNE

In Israel's early days, God instructed parents to teach their children about him and his ways (Deut. 4:9), and that's exactly what Asaph does in this psalm (vv. 1–8). His teaching is designed to showcase God's continual faithfulness to his people and to warn the younger generation not to repeat the sin patterns of their forefathers. He recounts several episodes from Israel's history, including the plagues God sent on Egypt (vv. 42–51), the exodus (v. 13), the miraculous provision of food, and God's guidance during their years in the wilderness (vv. 15–20, 23–29). Despite these many signs of God's love, his people rebelled against him when he allowed hardships to test their faith. The people "forgot" God, which means they chose to turn away in unbelief (v. 11). They remembered him only when he disciplined them severely (vv. 33–35). Even then, their repentance was largely superficial (vv. 36–37), as they turned repeatedly from God to idols, false gods they thought they could manipulate to serve them (v. 58). From their earliest days God's people grieved him (v. 40), provoked him to jealousy, and stirred up his anger (v. 58). Through it all, God's compassion and faithfulness never ceased, and he continued to care for them, raising up a shepherd-king to safeguard them in his ways (vv. 67–72).

MUSICAL NOTES
God's Grace
The history of Israel is actually the history of all God's people in every age, including us. We try to cast him off and go our own way, but he doesn't let us go. Rather than giving us what we deserve, he gives us the Good Shepherd to lead us back home to him (John 10:11; Rev. 7:14).

God's Attributes
- compassionate
- forgiving
- jealous
- merciful
- shepherding

SING THE SONG
Meditate on 2 Timothy 2:11–13.

Psalm

❧ 79 ❧

How Long, O Lord?

THEME

Sin and calamity go hand in hand, but God is faithful to deliver repentant people.

HARMONY

Asaph composed Psalm 79 to lament a calamity in Jerusalem, the special city where God dwelled with his people. Like other laments, Psalm 79 expresses perplexity, anguish, and discouragement, but to this psalm is added a frank acknowledgment of the sin that led to the disaster. Again we see that God welcomes boldness and honesty when we cry out to him, and we need not fear that he won't hear, because he has promised never to turn away from those who truly seek him.

SINGING IN TUNE

Defilement occurs when unholiness invades space set apart for God, whether a building (v. 1) or the human heart, and sin is always the entryway. God's house in Jerusalem, where God's people met to enjoy his presence, was attacked by unbelieving outsiders and destroyed, along with many of God's own people (vv. 1–4). Asaph knows full well that the invasion was God's way of clarifying that he will not allow unrepentant sin to drag on. That's why he pleads for atonement and deliverance (vv. 5, 8–9). Overarching the psalm is a plea that God will stop the invaders from doing further damage. Asaph asks God to lift his anger from his people and direct it instead toward the enemies—a bold request based solely on God's promise to show favor to those who belong to him (vv. 6, 10, 12). God's people have damaged his reputation through their sin, but God's overpowering of the enemy would serve to undo that damage (vv. 10, 12). As bad as things are, the people are confident that God will come to their aid, not because they deserve it but because he has pledged to shepherd them forever (v. 13).

MUSICAL NOTES

God's Grace

We cannot undo the damages wrought by sin, including the spiritual defilement it causes. God himself must make atonement, which he has done in full through the sacrifice of his Son on the cross. In him we are forgiven, cleansed, and restored, and nothing can remove God's favor from us.

God's Attributes

- faithful
- forgiving
- powerful
- purifying
- redeeming
- shepherding

SING THE SONG

Explain how 1 John 2:1–6 answers the plight of God's people expressed in Psalm 79.

Psalm

❧ 80 ❧

God's Vine

THEME

God disciplines his people when they sin so that they will turn back
to him.

HARMONY

Asaph composed Psalm 80 as a lament when God's people were suffering
the consequences of their unfaithfulness. Again we see that God welcomes boldness and honesty when we cry out to him, even when we are
responsible for our suffering, and that he will never turn away from those
who truly seek him.

SINGING IN TUNE

God's people wandered from him, forsaking a precious covenant relationship. But God never lets go of his people, so in order to win them
back, God removed his protection and allowed pagan enemies to do them
harm (vv. 4–6). Suffering under this divine discipline, they see their sin,
and they cry out to God for mercy. They long to be back in his protective
fellowship (vv. 17–18), which is exactly what God intends. God's work
with his people has always been like that of a gardener tending his vineyard (vv. 8–11), and he will patiently continue his cultivating work even
when wild grapes spring up, useless fruit not worth harvesting. When
the vine became useless in Asaph's day, God in his grief brought down
the walls that protected it (vv. 12–13; see also Isa. 5:1–7). Left vulnerable

and dying, the people ask God to remember his intentions and to restore his broken-down vineyard to fruitful life under his care as they wait for a sign of his favor (v. 19).

MUSICAL NOTES

God's Grace

God took great care in planting and cultivating the vine of his people, but despite his nurturing hand, the vineyard never flourished as God intended. That's why Jesus came—to be everything God's people failed to be—on our behalf. He is the true vine (John 15:1), and those grafted into him will produce the good fruit that God always intended.

God's Attributes

- holy
- merciful
- nurturing
- providing
- saving
- shepherding

SING THE SONG

Meditate on passages about God and his vineyard: Isaiah 5:1-7; Jeremiah 2:21; 12:10; Ezekiel 15:1-8; 17:7-10; and John 15:1-9.

Psalm

❧ 81 ☙

Listen and Love

THEME

Satisfaction is found only in walking with God.

HARMONY

Psalm 81 was composed by Asaph. The song contains a message directly from God. Such messages are called "oracles," and we see these most often in the writings of the prophets. For that reason, Psalm 81 can be called a "prophetic hymn."

SINGING IN TUNE

The song begins on a note of joyful worship (vv. 1–3) before turning to serious instruction, which shows that hearing any word from God, even hard words, is a privilege worthy of praise.[4] The people are reminded of all God has done for them over the years, freeing them from slavery in Egypt (vv. 5–6) and providing for their needs even when they complained against him in the wilderness (v. 7). The father heart of God pours out his desire for his children to trust him and obey rather than depend on idols—things or people that cannot provide what they need (vv. 8–9, 11). When God's people abandon him for idols, he eventually removes his protective hand and allows their hearts to become enslaved by lies (vv. 11–12). Even so, God pours out his love toward those who stray and grieves over their betrayals, all the while holding out fresh hope for blessing if they will only come home to him (vv. 13–16).

MUSICAL NOTES

God's Grace

God lovingly woos resistant people to come live under the protection of his fellowship. So great is his love that he takes the initiative, seeking even while he is not sought and saving those who have not first asked to be saved. No human love compares to this love, which God lavished on us most fully in sending his Son. "For while we were still weak, at the right time Christ died for the ungodly. For one will scarcely die for a righteous person—though perhaps for a good person one would dare even to die—but God shows his love for us in that while we were still sinners, Christ died for us" (Rom. 5:6–8).

God's Attributes

- fatherly
- gracious
- just
- loving
- satisfying

SING THE SONG

Consider how Jesus's parable in Luke 15:11–32 reflects what we see of God in Psalm 81.

Psalm

~ 82 ~

Justice Matters

THEME

World rulers are accountable to God, and he requires them to ensure just treatment for everyone under their authority.

HARMONY

Psalm 82 was composed by Asaph to lament community-wide injustice. The gods in the divine council (v. 1) are best understood as human beings.

SINGING IN TUNE

The majority of this world's rulers don't give much thought to God and his ways. As a result, much of what they decree springs from a craving for personal power, worldliness, and warped thinking rather than a desire for righteousness and justice (v. 5). The vulnerable in society typically suffer the most, which grieves the heart of God and violates his standards for human rulers (v. 2). Therefore, God will judge them for their selfishness and the harm it causes (vv. 1, 6–7). Nevertheless, there is hope. God, the ultimate ruler, will not fail, and he works through all injustice to accomplish his good purposes (v. 8).

MUSICAL NOTES

God's Grace

One way or another, every single ruler in Israel's history failed to live up to God's righteous standards. But the failures didn't surprise God or throw a curve ball in his plans. The failures were meant to make God's people yearn for more than any mere human ruler could ever provide, for a King who would bring about justice for all, not through force but through faith. Jesus is that ruler, the King of kings. No matter what we have to endure from the hands of unjust rulers now, we will live under his rule in his city of endless blessing for eternity.

God's Attributes

- compassionate
- judging
- powerful
- ruling

SING THE SONG

Christians are called to submit to civic authorities, yet not at the expense of obedience to God. Read Acts 5:27–32 and Romans 13:1–7. Ponder how those passages tie into Psalm 82.

Psalm

~~»» 83 ««~~

The God Who Conquers

THEME

No plot against God's people will ultimately prevail.

HARMONY

Psalm 83 is a lament composed by Asaph for all of God's people to sing during a national crisis. His song includes a prayer for enemy downfall. Asaph's request is driven not only by a desire for deliverance but also for the triumph of righteousness over evil.

SINGING IN TUNE

God's foes scheme and plot how to harm the community of God's people, and the threat is especially dangerous because these foes have joined forces to do harm (vv. 2–8). Asaph reflects on times when God powerfully thwarted death plots against his people (vv. 9–12), and he asks God to do the same thing again, rendering the evildoers ineffective and making them ashamed of their evil ways (vv. 13–17). Rescue isn't the psalmist's only motive, nor does his prayer spring from a vengeful spirit. His hope is that God will be glorified to those who have hated him (v. 18).

MUSICAL NOTES

God's Grace

When God sent Israel to take possession of the Promised Land, he instructed them to move in and destroy the people who lived there. God's instruction was rooted not in callous brutality but in grace. As his people took over the land, their testimony of God's saving greatness was spread, and many from those regions became believers. The conquest was designed to save. Rather than conquering lands today, believers conquer hearts by carrying out the Great Commission given by Jesus: "Go . . . and make disciples of all nations, baptizing them in the name of the Father and of the Son and of the Holy Spirit, teaching them to observe all that I have commanded you" (Matt. 28:19–20).

God's Attributes

- conquering
- saving

SING THE SONG

Read the story of Paul's conversion in Acts 9:1–19 and describe how a "theology of conquering" plays out in his story.

Psalm

⁓⁓ 84 ⁓⁓

Longing for the Lord

THEME

Life lived in fellowship with God is more delightful than life lived any other way.

HARMONY

Psalm 84 was composed by the Sons of Korah for God's people to sing while on a journey to Jerusalem to worship God. The Sons of Korah were appointed by King David to serve in music ministry in God's house. Travelers journeying there sang together to stir up joyful anticipation about entering God's presence and humble awe at being included in God's family.

SINGING IN TUNE

Israel had an overwhelming desire to be in God's house because that's where God's presence was most fully experienced in those days. They had learned that nothing is better than the delight of God's fellowship (vv. 1–2, 10). Enjoying God's company isn't just for a special few—all are welcome in God's house (vv. 3–4)—and those who know this joy will direct the overall course of their lives to dwell with him. In Israel's day, that often involved a tiring journey through the wilderness to get to the temple, but the joy that awaited them there propelled them through every obstacle (vv. 5–7). As people dwell in God's presence, they discover afresh that he is their light and protection and the giver of all that's good (vv. 11–12).

MUSICAL NOTES

God's Grace

"No good thing does he withhold from those who walk uprightly" (v. 11). The promise isn't for those who never sin; it's for all who pursue God wholeheartedly. And the good gifts God gives to those who delight in him come not as payment for their pursuit; he gives just because he loves to give. "If you then, who are evil, know how to give good gifts to your children," Jesus said, "how much more will your Father who is in heaven give good things to those who ask him!" (Matt. 7:11).

God's Attributes

- delighting
- illuminating
- protecting
- providing
- trustworthy

SING THE SONG

Psalm 84 links joy with strength (vv. 5–7). Consider how Nehemiah 8:1–12 expresses this link.

Psalm

~~~ 85 ~~~

The Mercy of God

THEME

God disciplines his people when they sin, but he is faithful to forgive and restore.

HARMONY

Lament psalms sometimes include an acknowledgment of sin. Such is the case in Psalm 85, which was composed by the Sons of Korah. Laments were prayerfully sung by individuals and other times by God's people as a whole, as we see here. Despite the sin underlying the lament, the people sing with confidence rather than fear because God is merciful and kind, and he responds to the cries of his people with love and deliverance. In Psalm 85, the people's confidence of forgiveness is rooted in Exodus 34:6–7, where God declares to Moses the merciful kindness of his character.

SINGING IN TUNE

When we turn from God to sin, he doesn't sit idly by and hope we get our spiritual act together. Instead, he allows us to suffer, sometimes by withholding something we need or by allowing us to fall into inescapably difficult circumstances. His intention is to get us to recognize our sin as *sin* so that we turn away from it and back to him. Israel recalls how God has worked this way in times past (vv. 1–3). They find themselves in similar straits once again, so they pray for fresh revival (vv. 4–7). They

192

are confident of forgiveness and of being restored to the fruitfulness of life in God's presence because God is faithful to keep his promises, even when they are not. Yet simply being sorry isn't enough. True repentance includes a heart-level determination not to sin in those ways again (vv. 8–13).

MUSICAL NOTES

God's Grace

Israel was confident of being forgiven because God had revealed himself through Moses as merciful. We have even more confidence because we know what underlies that mercy—the cross of Christ, where all our sins were paid for. All God's wrath against sin was poured out on his Son, so mercy is all that's left for those who take refuge in him. The cross is where God's righteousness "kissed" peace for all God's people in every age for all time (v. 10).

God's Attributes

- forgiving
- giving
- holy
- loving
- merciful
- providing
- righteous
- saving

SING THE SONG

Note the specific ways that Hosea 14:1–9 echoes Psalm 85.

Psalm

≫≫ 86 ≪≪

God's Unfailing Love

THEME

Confidence in God's character leads to boldness in prayer.

HARMONY

David composed Psalm 86 to lament his suffering, perhaps brought on in part by his own sin. The laments express perplexity, anguish, and even discouragement in the midst of overwhelming circumstances. Yet they also reflect the confident hope of those who trust their compassionate and faithful God. The psalms of lament teach us that God welcomes boldness and honesty when we cry out to him. We can be confident that he hears us, because he has promised never to turn away from those who seek him.

SINGING IN TUNE

David's closeness to the Lord is evident in how he prays. He asks for specific blessings, and for each one he gives a reason. Because David is needy, he asks God to listen (v. 1). Because he walks with God, he prays to be guarded on that path (v. 2). Because he clings to God, he asks for God's favor on his life (v. 3). Because he relies on God, he asks for a happy heart (v. 4). And he makes each of these requests because he knows that God is good, merciful, and loving to those who trust him (vv. 5–7). David knows that one day, everyone will bow before God—even those who hate him now—so whatever harm his enemies do is temporary at best (vv. 8–10, 14). David knows the Lord and that full, rich, abundant life is found only in fellowship with him, so he wants every hindrance to fellowship removed. That's why he prays that God would teach him and give him an undivided heart (v. 11). God is ready and willing to teach those who want not only to know him but to live out what they know. They "set" God before them in all they do (v. 14), and as they walk with him, they discover for themselves that God is all he has promised to be for his people.

MUSICAL NOTES

God's Grace

David in his prayer claims to be godly, but he wasn't talking about keeping the law perfectly. His godliness was about trusting God and living in conscious dependence on him. In the same way, God delights to answer our prayers when we come to him with nothing but our need, trusting not in ourselves but in his sufficiency to guide our path through the perplexities of life and the challenges of living as a disciple of Jesus.

God's Attributes

- forgiving
- giving
- gracious
- kind
- listening
- loving
- powerful

SING THE SONG

Outline how the instruction in James 1:5–8; 4:7–10 is woven through Psalm 86.

Psalm

~ 87 ~

Gathering In

THEME

God draws people from every nation to worship him.

HARMONY

Psalm 87 was composed by the Sons of Korah to celebrate God's love for Jerusalem, which was also called "Zion." The city was so special in those days because it's where God chose to reveal his presence, protection, and power to his people.

SINGING IN TUNE

It seems odd to us that God's people sang joyful songs about a city, but Jerusalem, or Zion, was no ordinary city. The temple was constructed there, and in the temple God met with his people. So Israel's joyful songs about Zion are really songs about God himself (vv. 1–3). What's surprising to us is that pagan nations—people who don't know God—are included in the song (v. 4), but they are included because the song is future oriented. God's people are rejoicing in their special calling as ambassadors of God to these outsiders. By means of their witness, outsiders are brought into the city, and it becomes their home too (vv. 5–6).

MUSICAL NOTES

God's Grace

From the time of Abraham, God intended to work through his people to call and gather others (Gen. 12:3). He has been fulfilling this intention ever since, as he weaves his people in and among nations and people groups who don't yet know him. God's good purposes are being worked through all the chaos that characterizes our world. "This mystery," says the apostle Paul, "is that the Gentiles are fellow heirs, members of the same body, and partakers of the promise in Christ Jesus through the gospel" (Eph. 3:6).

God's Attributes
- purposeful
- saving
- sovereign

SING THE SONG

Describe how Isaiah 49:5–7; Luke 24:44–47; Acts 13:44–49; and Galatians 3:7–9 show the fulfillment of Psalm 78.

Psalm

~~» 88 «~~

When the Way Is Dark

THEME

God is always with us in our suffering, even when he seems far off.

HARMONY

The Sons of Korah composed Psalm 88 as a lament. Like other laments, the song expresses perplexity, anguish, and even discouragement in the midst of overwhelming circumstances. It stands apart in the Psalter as the only psalm without a hopeful ending. Even so, we can be hopeful in the darkest of times because God has promised never to forsake his people.

SINGING IN TUNE

Suffering can be relentless. That describes the situation of the psalmist, who cries out to God day and night for relief (vv. 1–2). So intense is his suffering that he likens it to the approach of death (vv. 3–5). Worst of all, he feels deserted by God, and so great is his anguish that his friends can't help him; in fact, they can no longer bear even to be around him (vv. 8, 18). The psalmist knows that God controls everything that happens, so he recognizes that ultimately God is the source of his suffering (vv. 6–8, 16, 18). But that's not why he feels deserted by God. He feels abandoned because, despite his ceaseless pleas, he can't "find" God when he calls to him (v. 14). Nevertheless, the psalmist still trusts, which is evident from the fact that he continues to pray, and he knows that the One who has caused his suffering is the very One with the power to relieve it.

MUSICAL NOTES

God's Grace

The Puritans were frank about what they called "divine desertion," times when God deliberately withholds a sense of his nearness, and his intentions in it are counterintuitive—to bring us closer to him than we have ever been before.[5] And no matter how we feel, God has promised never to forsake us, because he forsook his Son instead. On the cross, Jesus was abandoned by God in our place, so to all who put their trust in him, God says, "I will never leave you nor forsake you" (Heb. 13:5).

God's Attributes

- faithful
- near
- sovereign

SING THE SONG

Identify specific imagery from Psalm 88 in the events before and during the crucifixion: Matthew 27:45–46; Mark 14:32–42; 66–72; and John 16:31–33.

Psalm

⚘ 89 ⚘

A Royal Blessing

THEME

When God's king flourishes, so do the people he governs.

HARMONY

Psalm 89 was composed by Ethan, a man renowned for great wisdom (1 Kings 4:29–31). His song is a lament, yet in it he also rejoices over the blessings of life under God's appointed line of kings, which began with David.

SINGING IN TUNE

Those who belong to God are privileged above all others on earth because they are the recipients of his love and faithfulness (vv. 1–2). God chose to work his blessings into his people's lives through a line of human kings (vv. 3–4), and he is able to do that because he is the Creator and ruler of everything (vv. 5–12). He is also righteous and loving (vv. 13–14), and life in him brings joy and stability (vv. 15–18). Through the appointed king, God fathers his people, and his parenting includes discipline when they stray from his ways (vv. 19–33). Yet even when they are unfaithful and suffer for it, God remains faithful and loving (vv. 33–37). Just as the people flourish under a righteous king, they suffer under an unfaithful one (vv. 38–45). Psalm 89 was composed at just this point, which is why the song's praise turns to a petition for relief and renewal (vv. 46–52).

MUSICAL NOTES

God's Grace

David and all the kings of Israel who followed him failed in their task to lead righteously, and their failures meant suffering for all. Nevertheless, God had promised to bless his people forever through this line of kings, and he has kept his promise through Jesus, the final descendant of David to take the throne. In every way that David and his descendants failed, Jesus succeeded. He is God's anointed, the King of kings, and in him we receive every promised blessing.

God's Attributes

- faithful
- fatherly
- kingly
- loving
- powerful
- sovereign

SING THE SONG

Read the apostle Paul's sermon in Acts 13:16–39 to deepen your grasp of the historical picture presented in Psalm 89.

The
PSALTER

Book 4

Psalm

❧ 90 ❧

Redeeming the Time

THEME

Life is short, so make the most of it by living in God's ways.

HARMONY

Moses composed Psalm 90 sometime during the forty years he led God's people through the wilderness. His song is basically a prayer for God's strength and encouragement to grapple with the hardships of life.

SINGING IN TUNE

God has no beginning or end. Unlike us, he has always been and always will be (vv. 1–3). And God isn't marked by time, as we are. He wove time into the fabric of creation when he separated night from day. Therefore, time is a created thing, and at the end of the ages, it will cease to exist (v. 4). For now, however, our lives are marked by time, and because of sin, ever since man's fall in the garden of Eden, each of us has very little of it (vv. 5–10). Aware of this reality, Moses petitions God. First, he asks God to bless his people with the wisdom to live well (v. 12). Second, in light of man's sinfulness, he prays for mercy (v. 13). Third, Moses prays for such an outpouring of God's love that his people won't be tempted to find satisfaction in the stuff of this life (v. 14). Fourth, he prays for revelation. He asks for spiritual sight to see God as he really is in all his glory (v. 16). Finally, he asks that God will enable his people to fulfill their calling, both as God's united family and as individuals (v. 17).

MUSICAL NOTES

God's Grace

The brevity of life is a terrifying prospect for those who don't know God. For them, this world, despite its many troubles, is all there is. The heart of wisdom Moses prays for is one rooted in an eternal perspective. Living with eternity in view enables us to maximize the gift of time each of us is given. Paradoxically, an eternal perspective frees us from the crushing burden of wringing all we can from this world. In the light of eternity, our accomplishments—and our choices about jobs and marriage and where to live—are relatively insignificant. The gift of wisdom enables us to realize that this world is not our home—God is (v. 1).

God's Attributes

- eternal
- loving
- purposeful
- satisfying

SING THE SONG

Describe how Paul's instructions in Ephesians 5:15–21 and in Colossians 4:5–6 serve as a sermon on Psalm 90.

Psalm

ᢒᢒᢒ 91 ᢨᢨᢨ

Shadow of the Almighty

THEME

God is a proven security for all who trust in him.

HARMONY

Psalm 91 was composed by an unknown writer to express confidence in God's care and protection, no matter what threatens.

SINGING IN TUNE

Abiding in God and trusting God go hand in hand. That's because the better we know him, the more we trust him (vv. 1–2). As we walk in the shelter of his Word and in the fellowship of other believers, he keeps us from danger (vv. 3–4), and those who live close to him aren't dominated by fear and anxiety, because they trust his providential governing of everything and everyone (vv. 5–8). God protects his own, even directing angels to guard their path (v. 11), and he equips them to overcome evil (v. 13). God desires a reciprocal love relationship with his people. As they cling to him, he protects; when they call on him, he answers; when troubles come, he delivers, and he will bring each one safely home to heaven (vv. 14–16).

MUSICAL NOTES

God's Grace

God is trustworthy—we are safe in him at all times. He is also strong, but his strength is no brute force. He is tender in his care, which is why he likens himself to a bird protecting her young under the warmth of her wings (v. 4).

God's Attributes
- delivering
- loving
- protecting
- trustworthy

SING THE SONG

Dwelling in the shelter of God entails living by God's Word in everything. Meditate on Luke 4:1–12, where Jesus demonstrated such reliance in the wilderness.

Psalm

❧ 92 ☙

A Joyful Day

THEME

God's people gather together to praise him for his powerful work in the world and in their own lives.

HARMONY

Many of the psalms were sung in celebration of God's greatness and the privileges that come to those who belong to him. These songs, called "praise psalms" and "thanksgiving psalms," were sung when Israel gathered for public worship. Psalm 92 was composed for joyful singing on the Sabbath.

SINGING IN TUNE

The way God works in the world is designed to bring joy to human beings and fill them with praise and thanksgiving (vv. 1–5), and walking in that way is how people flourish. Conversely, those who seek blessing in worldliness miss out on joy, and their flourishing is as fleeting as that of grass (vv. 6–9). The psalmist calls them stupid fools, which implies that God's joy-producing works aren't hidden from them—they simply refuse to see. Those who live for God find true happiness, because they become all God intended them to be. They flourish like mighty trees in God's presence, most especially as they live in the fellowship of other believers, and they are spiritually fruitful all the days of their lives (vv. 12–15).

MUSICAL NOTES

God's Grace

On the Sabbath, the last day of the week, God's people gathered to worship the Lord. It was a weekly celebration. Today we enjoy that privilege on the Lord's Day, the first day of the week. God has given us one whole day in seven to set aside our work and our daily cares to focus on him and enjoy his company in the presence of other believers. And God has structured this setting, the church, to be the place of our flourishing (see, for example, Acts 2:42–47; Eph. 3:7–10).

God's Attributes

- giving
- praiseworthy
- prospering
- renewing
- strengthening

SING THE SONG

Describe how Mark 2:23–28 adds a note of celebration to the Sabbath.

$\mathcal{P}salm$

❧❧ 93 ❧❧

The King of Creation

THEME

God the Creator rules everything he created.

HARMONY

A few of the psalms were composed to rejoice in God as King. Psalm 93 focuses on God as the King of all creation.

SINGING IN TUNE

Waves of the sea bring to mind fun-filled summer vacations, but in the ancient world, these majestic waters represented uncontrollable danger. Yet the God who created the seas is well able to control them (vv. 3–4). God's people need not fear any threat from nature or anything else on earth, because God rules it all (vv. 1–2), and as they walk in his ways, they can trust that he governs everything for the benefit of his people (v. 5). The book of Revelation tells us that one day, in the new earth, there will be no more sea (Rev. 21:1), but this doesn't mean there won't be any oceans or large bodies of water. It means that there won't be any more chaos of any kind. Until that day, God sets his limits on the chaos of nature and on the overwhelming circumstances that befall our own lives.

MUSICAL NOTES

God's Grace

The Lord Jesus got into a boat one day, and his disciples came along with him. Out at sea a storm arose. The disciples panicked, but not Jesus. In fact, he slept through the tossing waves. When the disciples frantically woke him, he challenged their weak faith and calmed the storm with a word (Matt. 8:23–26). Jesus led them *into* the storm for the very purpose of getting them *out* of it, thereby revealing himself as the fulfillment of Psalm 93, the Savior of all who trust in him, the calmer of storms.

God's Attributes

- creating
- holy
- ruling
- sovereign

SING THE SONG

Jesus led his disciples into stormy seas on more than one occasion. Read what happened in Matthew 14:22–33 and trace what you see there to Psalm 93 and the story in Matthew 8:23–26.

Psalm

❧ 94 ❧

Kept from All Evil

THEME

Afflicted by those who hold the Lord in low regard, God's people pray for protection and deliverance.

HARMONY

Psalm 94 is a lament that expresses the confidence God's people have in times of trouble. No one can harm them without God's say-so. The song includes a note of vengeance, but the intent is a desire for deliverance and for the triumph of righteousness over evil. Psalm 94 shows us how to pray when evil threatens or tempts us to unbelief.

SINGING IN TUNE

It's not wrong to pray for justice. In fact, it's good and right to pray that evil won't succeed and that God's ways will prove superior to all who see (vv. 1–2). We can be sure that one day God will judge all injustice, but in the meantime God allows it and makes use of it for his own good purposes (vv. 3–4). Especially heinous in God's eyes is the oppression of the weak and needy by arrogant people who believe they can get away with it (vv. 5–7). Such evildoers are fools. Indulging in sin has dulled their spiritual senses, blinding them to the reality that God sees and knows what they are doing (vv. 8–11). The psalmist realizes that God is at work in present difficulties to grow and strengthen the faith of his troubled people, something that wise people recognize as a blessing (vv. 12–15).

At times, God strips away every vestige of human help to teach us to lean more fully on him, and as we do, we discover that he is more than sufficient to protect and sustain us (vv. 16–22). Those who refuse to embrace God find destruction rather than deliverance, and they will discover that apart from the Lord, what goes around, comes around (v. 23).

MUSICAL NOTES

God's Grace

Fools shut their hearts to God and are led deeper and deeper into despair and destruction. This is God's judgment. But destruction is never the outcome for those who trust in him, who believe that Christ paid for their sin on the cross. For all who believe, God's purposes in trials are redemptive, not destructive. Trials are his discipline and a sign not of anger but of fatherly love (Prov. 3:11–12; Heb. 12:5–8).

God's Attributes

- defending
- fatherly
- just
- protecting
- upholding
- wise

SING THE SONG

Describe what Hebrews 12:3–29 adds to your understanding of Psalm 94.

Psalm

❧ 95 ☙

Blessed Rest

THEME

Trusting in God and walking in his ways is the only path to blessing.

HARMONY

Psalm 95 was composed as a teaching tool. Those who sang it were strengthened to walk faithfully with God as they looked back on some painful times in Israel's history. The background of Psalm 95 is found in Exodus 17:1–7 and Numbers 14:1–30.

SINGING IN TUNE

God's rule over creation is cause for joy because he governs it for the prosperity of his people (vv. 1–6). God takes special note of his own and guides them as a shepherd tends his sheep (v. 7). In that way, he deepens their trust in him, which in turn leads them to praise and obedience. As we, his people, "worship and bow down" (v. 6), in other words, as we approach God with humility, our eyes see clearly and our hearts stay soft. Rejecting his ways, his ordering of our lives, does the opposite—it blinds our eyes and hardens our hearts, and if we continue along that course, we cut ourselves off from God's gracious care. That's what happened in the days of Moses, when Israel wandered in the desert. The people chafed against God's leading and grumbled that his provision was insufficient. Over time, God's patience ran out, and the discontented generation died out in the wilderness (vv. 7–11).

MUSICAL NOTES

God's Grace

Complaining is the mark of a discontented heart, and over time such a heart grows hard in unbelief and cannot participate in the "rest" (v. 11) that comes from walking with God in trustful obedience. Going our own way always proves unsettling, and we never find the rest we're looking for. True rest is held out to us in Jesus, the One who says, "Come to me, all who labor and are heavy laden, and I will give you rest. Take my yoke upon you, and learn from me, for I am gentle and lowly in heart, and you will find rest for your souls. For my yoke is easy, and my burden is light" (Matt. 11:28–30).

God's Attributes

- creating
- fatherly
- kingly
- providing
- shepherding

SING THE SONG

Review the story of Israel in the wilderness in Numbers 14:1–30. Note why you think the psalmist recalls it here in Psalm 95.

Psalm

❧ 96 ☙

Come and Worship!

THEME

The whole world declares the fame of God's name.

HARMONY

Psalm 96 was composed as a hymn to rejoice in God as King of creation and to call all people to come and worship him.

SINGING IN TUNE

This missions-oriented psalm calls all people, not just God's own, to see him for who he is, praise him for it, and spread the knowledge of him in every place. God's fame is spread not only by proclamation of who he is, but by the manner in which he is proclaimed—joyful song, displays of nature, awe-filled worship, and gladness of heart (vv. 1–3, 7–9, 10–12). Outsiders, the Gentiles, can forget about the false gods they worship and join the company of God's people in singing, because only the Lord is worthy of praise (v. 5). He alone is majestic, holy, and gloriously strong (vv. 6–7), and these divine qualities produce gladness of heart because God works them on behalf of those who love him. He is ruler of all, and he weaves his righteousness all through his creation (vv. 10, 13). Everyone and everything are invited to participate, and as God's attributes are proclaimed and praised, others will surely come to know him and join the joyful song.

MUSICAL NOTES

God's Grace

God never intended to reveal himself only to Israel, a select few; rather, he intended to reveal himself *through* Israel to the whole world. Such is the calling of all God's people in every age—to declare his glory and to make him known so that outsiders will be brought in. Were it left up to us, we wouldn't sing joyfully about missions, because we often fail in our witness, as Israel did time and again. But God's intentions are never ruined by the failures of his people. It wasn't the "new song" of Israel that accomplished God's plan to gather a great multitude for his family, but the new song of the Lamb: "Worthy are you to take the scroll and to open its seals, for you were slain, and by your blood you ransomed people for God from every tribe and language and people and nation, and you have made them a kingdom and priests to our God, and they shall reign on the earth" (Rev. 5:9–10).

God's Attributes

- creating
- glorious
- holy
- intentional
- kingly
- majestic
- righteous

SING THE SONG

Consider how Isaiah 11:1–9 ties in with Psalm 96.

Psalm

⚕ 97 ⚕

God Most High

THEME

Because God rules his creation, evil will not prevail.

HARMONY

Psalm 97 is another hymn that rejoices in God as King of creation. The emphasis in this song is God's inevitable victory over every false god.

SINGING IN TUNE

The power of idols is the illusion that they can be controlled. A god that will bless but not restrict—it's what the human heart naturally craves. That's why false gods are initially so enticing, but the appeal lasts only until their enslaving, destructive nature is exposed (v. 7). The one and only God, the Lord of the universe, cannot be controlled. He proved this when he veiled his glory on Mount Sinai in clouds (v. 2), and he proves it whenever he showcases his power in nature (vv. 4–5). The humble in heart submit rather than rebel, and they find joy in serving the one true Lord (vv. 8–9). But God wants more from his people than awe—he wants their love, and living in the light of this love relationship breeds hatred for evil and gratitude for righteousness (vv. 10–12).

MUSICAL NOTES

God's Grace

The light God provides to the righteous in verse 10 has to do with guidance. Even though he shrouded himself in dark clouds, he lit the path of his people along ways broad and joy-filled rather than narrow and restrictive. At the coming of Jesus, the darkness that hid God's glory was forever lifted. "I am the light of the world," he said. "Whoever follows me will not walk in darkness, but will have the light of life" (John 8:12).

God's Attributes

- creating
- glorious
- holy
- mysterious
- ruling

SING THE SONG

Describe how Exodus 19:1–25 was incorporated into Psalm 97 and explain why the details of the exodus story set the tone for the psalm.

Psalm

~~~ 98 ~~~

Joy to the World

THEME

The whole world is called to praise God for his wondrous works.

HARMONY

Psalm 98 rejoices in God as King of creation. This celebratory hymn emphasizes God's powerful, visible work on behalf of his people.

SINGING IN TUNE

Joyful song inevitably fills the heart of all who realize that salvation comes only from the Lord (v. 1), and he makes his saving grace known to the whole world as he works in and through the lives of those who love him (vv. 2–3). Israel rejoices at the high privilege of being God's ambassador and the instrument of his salvation to the surrounding nations, and they carry out their calling with songs of praise so that all might enjoy the blessings of life under the divine King (vv. 4–6). Even nature—rivers and hills—is a divinely appointed ambassador—every created thing points to its Creator (vv. 8–9).

MUSICAL NOTES

God's Grace

The rejoicing of those who first sang this psalm foreshadows an even greater joy—the coming of Christ Jesus. At his coming, the effects of sin on the whole earth began to turn around, and because Jesus bore the curse for sin, the renewal that began with his birth will continue until his return, when all things will be restored and will perfectly reflect their Creator. In the meantime, the mission of Psalm 98 continues as "the creation waits with eager longing for the revealing of the sons of God. For the creation was subjected to futility, not willingly, but because of him who subjected it, in hope that the creation itself will be set free from its bondage to corruption and obtain the freedom of the glory of the children of God" (Rom. 8:19–21).

God's Attributes
- faithful
- loving
- purposeful
- restoring
- saving
- sovereign

SING THE SONG

Describe what Isaiah 11:1–10 adds to your understanding of Psalm 98.

Psalm

❧ 99 ❧

Holy Is He!

THEME

God's holiness when rightly understood evokes awe and praise.

HARMONY

Psalm 99 was composed as a hymn to rejoice in God as King of all creation. This song emphasizes the purity and wonder of his holiness.

SINGING IN TUNE

The Lord is high above his creation, separated by his holiness—his divine perfection—from all he has made, yet he shows mercy to sinful human beings by separating out certain people in whom he works his perfect righteousness, justice, and truth (vv. 1–5). God's sitting on the cherubim (v. 1) indicates his merciful presence with his people. Those who receive his mercy and enjoy his perfect rule can only praise him in awe, especially because he invites sinners to draw near to him in prayer, and he answers them, forgiving their sin and conforming them to his holy character (vv. 6–8).

MUSICAL NOTES

God's Grace

For a perfectly holy God to show mercy to sinful people, atonement must be made. A life is required, since death is the just punishment for sin. In the psalmist's day, God accepted the life of an animal as atonement, and when its blood was brought to the ark and placed on the cover, the sinner was considered cleansed—until the next sin was committed, and then the ritual had to be done all over again. Ultimately, the sacrificial system was insufficient, "for it is impossible for the blood of bulls and goats to take away sins" (Heb. 10:4). The insufficiency of that old system was actually its very purpose—to show the need for something better than animal blood. It pointed to Jesus. "When Christ had offered for all time a single sacrifice for sins, he sat down at the right hand of God. . . . For by a single offering he has perfected for all time those who are being sanctified" (Heb. 10:12–14).

God's Attributes

- holy
- merciful
- sovereign

SING THE SONG

Learn about the origins of the ark of the covenant and the mercy seat from Exodus 25:1–22.

$\mathcal{P}_{\text{salm}}$

⤜⤜ 100 ⤛⤛

Come into His Presence

THEME

God's goodness to his people deserves praise and thanksgiving.

HARMONY

Many of the psalms were sung in celebration of God's greatness and the privileges that come to those who belong to him. These songs, called "praise psalms" and "thanksgiving psalms," were sung when Israel gathered for public worship, and included in many of them, such as here in Psalm 100, is an invitation to outsiders to turn to God and worship him too.

SINGING IN TUNE

The psalmist calls the entire world to a three-part response to the Lord as King and Creator: he is to be praised, served, and approached (vv. 1–2). To that is added a call to God's own people: "Know that the LORD, he is God!" (v. 3). God has revealed himself to his people, so they are to take advantage of that special privilege and make him their focus. As they do, they are reminded of their special status as those whom God guides, protects, and provides for. Believers are to give thanks individually, of course, but here in the psalm they are called to do it corporately, together with other believers, in God's house (v. 4). Gathered as one body, they praise and thank God for his overarching goodness, his unfailing love, and his ongoing faithfulness (v. 5).

MUSICAL NOTES

God's Grace

God demonstrates his love in countless ways. He guides our path, provides for our needs, forgives our sins, and delivers us from evil on a daily
basis—just because he is good. "Every good gift and every perfect gift is
from above, coming down from the Father of lights, with whom there is
no variation or shadow due to change" (James 1:17). He has already given
us the best gift of all—his Son, Jesus—through whom we are guaranteed
that his goodness toward us will continue for all time.

God's Attributes

- creating
- faithful
- loving
- providing
- shepherding

SING THE SONG

We thank God for providing our material needs, but he deserves our
thanks for so much more. Deepen your gratitude through what you find
in Romans 6:17; 1 Corinthians 15:56–57; Colossians 3:16–17; 1 Thessalonians 5:18; and 2 Thessalonians 1:3.

Psalm

⊰⊱ 101 ⊰⊱

Walking with God

THEME

A true disciple pursues righteousness and avoids evil.

HARMONY

Psalm 101 is a reflection on the attributes of a godly king. Psalms that focus on the king are often called "royal psalms." God appointed a line of kings, beginning with David, to lead his people in his paths. And God promised that through this line would come his greatest blessings (see 2 Sam. 7:12–17). Sure enough, when the kings served faithfully, all the people were blessed. But ultimately they were all failures in faithfulness. Even so, the people rejoiced in their king, which can mean only one thing—despite the royal failures, there was still hope. Human kings fail, but the divine God does not. He always keeps his promises.

SINGING IN TUNE

King David loved God, and because of that, he loved God's righteous paths. He so delights in the ways of righteousness that he sets his love to music (v. 1). Much as he loves God's ways, David still sins, so he determines to situate his life to better live out what he believes. First, he focuses on the ways of the Lord, and then he asks God to draw near (v. 2). David also commits to a life of integrity, both in public and in private (vv. 3–4). Such commitment entails avoiding temptation and the company of those who pursue sinful paths. As king of Israel, he also vows to root out sin in the community of God's people, and in so doing, he is acting on God's behalf (vv. 5, 8). As he rids the community of evil, he promotes righteousness by elevating the godly (vv. 6–7). Of course, David failed to live up to the standards he set in his song, which means his song points to a different king—the coming Messiah.

MUSICAL NOTES

God's Grace

David used his kingly authority to establish righteousness by means of reward and punishment—external means. Under King Jesus, righteousness is established internally as the Holy Spirit transforms hearts. When Jesus rose from the dead and ascended to heaven, the Holy Spirit came in a special new way to indwell all who believe so that now, "if the Spirit of him who raised Jesus from the dead dwells in you, he who raised Christ Jesus from the dead will also give life to your mortal bodies through his Spirit who dwells in you" (Rom. 8:11).

God's Attributes

- holy
- loving
- righteous
- transforming

SING THE SONG

Describe the ways in which Ephesians 1:3–14 shows the fulfillment of Psalm 101.

$\mathcal{P}_{salm}$

❧ 102 ❧

God Hears

THEME

God hears the cries of his people and comes to their aid.

HARMONY

Psalm 102 is a lament that expresses perplexity, anguish, and even discouragement in the midst of overwhelming circumstances. As with most laments in the Psalter, this song is overlaid with the confident hope of those who trust a compassionate and faithful God. The psalms of lament teach us that God welcomes boldness and honesty when we cry out to him, and we need not fear that he won't hear, because he has promised never to turn away from those who truly seek him.

SINGING IN TUNE

In deep distress, the suffering psalmist cries out to God, who seems distant and removed from the psalmist's plight (vv. 1–2). So intense is his suffering that it is taking a physical toll as well. He struggles to eat and sleep, and his pain is intensified by isolation and grief. To top it off, he is nagged by the thought that God is punishing him in anger (vv. 3–11). All this he pours out to the Lord, and then he turns the focus of his prayer from his suffering to the Lord himself, who has always proven to be faithful and has promised never to forsake his people. As the psalmist focuses on God's faithfulness, he is emboldened to ask for an immediate outworking of those promises (vv. 12–13). He bases his appeal on the special calling of God's people to bear witness about God's goodness to outsiders (vv. 15–16). He appeals also to the character of the Lord, who listens to the cries of those who call on him for help (v. 17). The psalmist doesn't know how his difficulty will turn out, and it has already proven costly. Yet even though his life—and all of creation—is unstable, God never changes, so those who trust in him are secure (vv. 23–28).

MUSICAL NOTES

God's Grace

God has never failed his people, even when they fail him. He is true to his character. "If we are faithless, he remains faithful—for he cannot deny himself" (2 Tim. 2:13). He will never stop listening to the cries of his own and coming to their rescue, and we are confident of this because of Christ our Savior, who is "the same yesterday and today and forever" (Heb. 13:8). In him is our hope.

God's Attributes

- attentive
- faithful
- sovereign
- unchanging

SING THE SONG

Read Jesus's parable of the persistent widow (Luke 18:1–8) and note what it adds to your understanding of Psalm 102.

Psalm

⤜ 103 ⤛

Remember God's Benefits

THEME

The faithful covenant Lord blesses his people in every conceivable way.

HARMONY

Psalm 103 was composed by David to celebrate God's greatness and the special privileges that are granted to God's people. Such songs, called "praise psalms" and "thanksgiving psalms," were sung when Israel gathered for public worship. Psalm 103 looks back on God's faithfulness to his people since the time of creation.

SINGING IN TUNE

David's love for the Lord shines all through his song. Here we find no requests—there is nothing but praise. To "bless" the Lord is to acknowledge his worth and proclaim his attributes, and David does this wholeheartedly (v. 1) as he calls God's people to be constantly mindful of their privileges (vv. 1–2). God forgives sin and heals its destructive effects (v. 3). In love and mercy, he brings good out of evil (v. 4). Chasing the superficial prizes of the world diminishes well-being, but a life lived for the Lord brings satisfaction (v. 5). The Lord fights for his people when they are helpless, and he does for them what they cannot do for themselves (vv. 6–7). God is patient with sinners who trust in his mercy, and like a compassionate father, he disciplines in love rather than punishes in anger (vv. 8–14). God's commitment to his people will never change;

he will always prove himself faithful, and because he controls the world and everyone in it, nothing can hinder his promise to bless those who fear his name (vv. 17–19).

MUSICAL NOTES

God's Grace

Because of sin, God could justly withhold from his people all the benefits David lists. Instead, he dissociates us from our sin—"as far as the east is from the west" (v. 12)—in order to shower all these benefits on us. Such love far exceeds that of even the most selfless human heart. A just and righteous God can love us in such tangible ways because when he removed our transgressions, he placed them on his Son instead. Jesus bore the punishment we deserve so that we can get the benefits he deserves.

God's Attributes

- compassionate
- forgiving
- generous
- giving
- kind
- loving
- merciful
- powerful
- saving

SING THE SONG

Describe how Ephesians 1:3–14 paints an even fuller picture of God's blessings.

$\mathcal{P}_{\!s}alm$

◈◈◈ 104 ◈◈◈

Majesty Made Known

THEME

God's power and goodness overshadow everything in creation.

HARMONY

Many of the psalms were sung in celebration of God's greatness and the privileges that come to those who belong to him. These songs, called "praise psalms" and "thanksgiving psalms," were composed primarily for singing when Israel gathered for public worship. Psalm 104 is based on the creation account in Genesis 1:2–2:3.

SINGING IN TUNE

God created the universe with his powerful majesty, and he continues to rule even its tiniest details with wisdom and might. Every created thing has a divinely appointed purpose. Bodies of water ebb and flow to provide sustenance and shelter for even the most insignificant of God's creatures, and food grows from the ground to nourish people and bring them joy. God's creation of night and day and the changing of seasons provide a satisfying rhythm to life (vv. 1–26). God works through his creation to reveal himself as the all-sufficient provider; every creature is dependent on him for survival (vv. 27–30). The psalmist concludes with a commitment to lifelong praise and a prayer that the evil that mars God's handiwork will cease (vv. 31–35).

MUSICAL NOTES

God's Grace

God's work in creation isn't arbitrary; skies and stars, mountains and oceans, storms and sunshine—God reveals himself to man through his handiwork, and he never ceases, even when people reject all he gives them to see. Glimpses of his glory and majesty are everywhere. The apostle Paul says that God "did not leave himself without witness, for he did good by giving you rains from heaven and fruitful seasons, satisfying your hearts with food and gladness" (Acts 14:17). And all God's work on earth—and in our own lives—is purposefully designed to draw us to him (Acts 17:24–27).

God's Attributes

- caring
- creating
- glorious
- powerful
- providing
- righteous
- sustaining

SING THE SONG

Describe how John 1:1–5 and Colossians 1:15–17 deepen your understanding of Psalm 104.

$\mathcal{P}salm$

~~~ 105 ~~~

Remembering

THEME

Reflecting on the mighty works of our promise-keeping God promotes praise and deepens our faith.

HARMONY

Psalm 105 is a historical psalm because it recounts God's past work in the lives of his people. The song reflects on God's promises to the patriarchs in Genesis and his dealings with his people in the book of Exodus. It was composed to instill gratitude and godly confidence in those who sing it.

SINGING IN TUNE

Children learn the alphabet by singing it, because songs help them remember. That's what the psalmist does as he sets to music God's rescuing, redeeming work in times past. By singing this song, God's people not only call to mind reasons for praise; they also spread God's fame to those who don't yet glory in his name. Glorying in God's name is to enjoy him in all the ways he has promised to be for his people (vv. 1–6). God is faithful every moment of every day, even when he leads his people into trying and painful situations. He guided Israel into the Promised Land (vv. 12–15, 43–44), provided food during famine (vv. 16–22), overruled their suffering as slaves in Egypt (vv. 23–38), and sustained them in the wilderness (vv. 39–42). God was present with his people and was controlling every event all those years. As they "remember the wondrous works that he has done" (v. 5), their hearts are encouraged to trust that God will continue to care for his own in every circumstance for all time.

MUSICAL NOTES

God's Grace

When God called Abraham to establish a people for himself, he made a promise, a covenant, to provide for their needs, guide them with his presence, and protect them with his love. And even though Israel failed to keep the covenant, God remained faithful to his promise. He keeps that promise still today through the finished work of Christ, whose life, death, and resurrection secured every imaginable blessing and the promise of God's presence forever.

God's Attributes

- delivering
- faithful
- intentional
- providing
- sovereign
- sustaining

SING THE SONG

For each historic episode recorded in Psalm 105, note the particular words the psalmist uses to describe God's work in the event and how his description shapes your view of God.

Psalm

❧ 106 ❧

The Inexhaustible Goodness of God

THEME

God remains faithful to unfaithful people.

HARMONY

Psalm 106 recalls God's work in the lives of his people, continuing the historical recap of Psalm 105.

SINGING IN TUNE

The longer we walk with God, the more of his goodness we see. That's what the psalmist sings about as he recounts the recurrent sin patterns of God's people and God's faithfulness to deliver them time and again from messes of their own making. At times we rebel against God when his ways with us don't meet our personal expectations. We believe he loves us, but our understanding of how he loves is often warped. Unbroken peace, prosperity, and pleasant circumstances are what we expect, and when he doesn't work that way in our lives, we turn from him. That's what God's people have always done, from the early days of Israel. Yet God delivers them because he keeps his promises (vv. 6–8). His deliverances often include painful discipline, because the pain works to restore the hearts of wayward people. And his discipline sometimes includes giving people what they crave in order to show them what they really need (vv. 13–15). When we want God to be something other than who he is, we set up other gods in his place—things or people we think we can manipulate in order to get our needs met. But it never works; in fact, idol worship takes away much more than it gives, and those who bow to idols risk eventual destruction (vv. 34–42). Because God is faithful, even when we are not, he delivers his people from their own destructions, and he does it again and again (vv. 43–44). God's faithfulness toward his people teaches us that sin never delivers what it promises and that God's love is way better than we ever imagined (v. 48).

MUSICAL NOTES

God's Grace

Contrary to what we deserve, God never gives up on his people. This is the essence of grace, which God demonstrated most fully in Christ. He bore the wrath we deserve so that we can experience the favor he deserves, and for that reason, "where sin increased, grace abounded all the more" (Rom. 5:20).

God's Attributes

- fatherly
- gracious
- merciful
- redeeming
- rescuing
- loving

SING THE SONG

Read one or more of the stories highlighted in Psalm 106 and note how each one deepens your understanding of sin and the character of God: Exodus 32:1–14; Numbers 14:1–24; 20:2–13; 25:1–15; Judges 2:11–3:6.

The
PSALTER

Book 5

$\mathcal{P}salm$

❧ 107 ☙

God's Steadfast Love

THEME

God never fails to deliver and restore his people.

HARMONY

Psalm 107 was composed as both a historical psalm and a psalm of thanksgiving. The backstory of Psalm 107 is the return of God's people from exile in Babylon.

SINGING IN TUNE

For years the prophets had warned God's people to trust in the Lord for safety rather than rely on ungodly foreign powers, but they refused, so the prophecies came true—God's people were carried away captive to pagan Babylon, where they were forced to assimilate into a worldly culture. Oh, how they missed their homeland! In time, God brought them home and restored them to prosperity and religious freedom, and that's what Psalm 107 celebrates (vv. 1–3). The song highlights four situations of suffering and God's deliverance in each case. The first concerns homeless exiles suffering the deprivations of the desert. When they cried out in their misery, God guided them out of the desert, back to the comforts of home and community (vv. 4–9). The second situation concerns the suffering brought on by rebellion. Sin has consequences, sometimes very painful ones, and it is God himself who leads us into them to teach us not to stray again. But that same God delivers those who cry out to him, and he restores them from the prisons of their own making (vv. 10–16). The third situation involves fools, those who disregard God's ways in favor of their own, which inevitably leads to destruction. However, even fools can cry out to God for relief and healing, and he is faithful to provide it (vv. 17–22). The fourth situation concerns people going about their regular business, in this case, on the sea. God calls forth a storm and then calms the storm when his terrified people cry for help (vv. 23–32). The response to all four deliverances is, "Let them thank the LORD for his steadfast love, for his wondrous works to the children of men!" (vv. 8, 15, 21, 31). God shows his goodness, mercy, and power in reversals of all kinds (vv. 33–42).

MUSICAL NOTES

God's Grace

The Lord of reversals is always at work to redeem, restore, and transform. What he did for the exiles in Israel, he still does today, most especially in the hearts of sinful people. "Now the Lord is the Spirit, and where the Spirit of the Lord is, there is freedom. And we all, with unveiled face, beholding the glory of the Lord, are being transformed into the same image from one degree of glory to another. For this comes from the Lord who is the Spirit" (2 Cor. 3:17–18).

God's Attributes

- good
- loving
- restoring
- revealing
- reversing

SING THE SONG

Describe how Psalm 107 is echoed in Mark 5:1–20; John 18:25–27; 21:15–19; and Acts 9:1–19.

Psalm

⁓≫ 108 ⤙⤙

Our Victory in God's Hands

THEME

God is faithful to preserve his people in every trouble.

HARMONY

Psalm 108 is a lament for the whole community to sing. David made use of material in Psalms 57 and 60 to compose this song.

SINGING IN TUNE

Israel's enemies have gained a foothold, and God seems absent. Nevertheless, David isn't shaken by the crisis, because he knows God is faithful and has committed to love his people (vv. 1–4). In this specific situation, David's confidence rests in God's long-ago promise to give his people the land of Canaan—the Promised Land—and to defeat those who try to stop them (vv. 7–9). So he prays the promise, asking God to show his hand and bring it to fulfillment (vv. 5–6). God's promise and David's prayer for its fulfillment are rooted not in heartlessness toward the enemies but in the desire that the "peoples" and "nations" would see the true God, one who delivers on his promises (v. 3). Despite the current crisis and its grim outlook, David looks beyond the circumstances and focuses on all he knows about God, which is why he concludes his song on a note of hope (vv. 12–13).

MUSICAL NOTES

God's Grace

Although David languishes in his difficulty, his trust doesn't waver. From him we see that lamenting our troubles doesn't negate our trust; in fact, honest realism about our difficulties, when taken to the Lord in prayer, opens the door to greater trust. Along with that comes hope, which grows as we look at the Lord more intensely than we look at our trouble. From that perspective, we get a big-picture view of God's big-picture purposes in all our troubles—to gather us together with others to enjoy his love and blessings for eternity.

God's Attributes

- faithful
- hope-giving
- loving
- purposeful
- rescuing

SING THE SONG

Describe how Romans 15:8–13 deepens your understanding of God's purposes as revealed in Psalm 108.

$\mathcal{P}\!salm$

~~>> 109 <<~~

Vindicated

THEME

God will right every injustice in his perfect way and time.

HARMONY

David composed Psalm 109 as a lament. It includes a lengthy prayer for the downfall of his persecutors. "Imprecatory laments" such as this were motivated by a desire not only for rescue but also for the triumph of righteousness over evil.

SINGING IN TUNE

Persecution by strangers is hard enough to bear, but when it comes from someone we love, the hurt is devastating. David is suffering that hurt, so he turns to the Lord for deliverance (vv. 1–5). Most of the psalm is taken up with David's prayer for the downfall of his persecutor (vv. 6–20), a request that doesn't seem loving or godly. But Jesus himself declared a similar fate on the scribes and Pharisees of his day (Matt. 23:1–36), and from both cases, we learn that calling for the destruction of evil isn't wrong. No matter how God determines to deal with the wicked, David trusts that God will deliver him (vv. 21–29) because God has a special care for the oppressed, especially those among his own people (vv. 30–31).

MUSICAL NOTES

God's Grace

David's suffering at the hand of a friend foreshadows Jesus's suffering at the hands of some whom he had loved, most especially Judas, who betrayed Jesus for money. In fact, the apostle Peter applies David's words, "May another take his office" (v. 8), to Judas (see Acts 1:20). Jesus experienced rejection, betrayal, and a level of hatred that David never did, yet "God has highly exalted him and bestowed on him the name that is above every name, so that at the name of Jesus every knee should bow, in heaven and on earth and under the earth, and every tongue confess that Jesus Christ is Lord, to the glory of God the Father" (Phil. 2:9–11). Through his vindication, ours is guaranteed.

God's Attributes

- defending
- judging
- protecting
- righteous

SING THE SONG

Read Luke 22:14–23, 47–53 and Acts 1:12–26 and describe how the theme of Psalm 109 worked out in the life of Judas.

$\mathcal{P}\!salm$

ϟϟϟ 110 ϡϡϡ

King of Kings

THEME

God's Son will be both King and priest.

HARMONY

David composed Psalm 110 as a "royal psalm." These songs were designed to focus the believing community on the vital role that Israel's kings played in God's plan to provide for his people and, most of all, to celebrate God himself as King. Some royal psalms, such as Psalm 110, are "messianic"—they point clearly to Jesus, the coming King of kings.

SINGING IN TUNE

Even as God's appointed king over Israel, David knew that a greater King—one of his own descendants—would one day come, as God had promised. This coming King would rule the entire world, and his own people would happily serve him (vv. 1–3). The One to come would be not only the greatest King but also the greatest priest. Both were needed—a king to ensure that God's people were protected by righteousness and a priest to provide access to God. The mysterious man Melchizedek (v. 4) was both king and priest, but he didn't fit the Old Testament kingly requirement—he wasn't related to David. That's how we know that Psalm 110 is really about Jesus. He is the only king from the family of David who also served as priest, fully bridging the sin gap between God and sinful people. He is therefore the only king who can truly bless those who serve him while retaining his rule over the whole world (vv. 5–7).

MUSICAL NOTES

God's Grace

No human king could ever meet the deepest needs of his people, because those needs involve deliverance from sin. Only King Jesus can lead his people into God's paths of blessing, and because he was sinless, the sacrifice he made for his people's sin—his very own self—keeps them there, in God's presence. "He is able to save to the uttermost those who draw near to God through him, since he always lives to make intercession for them" (Heb. 7:25).

God's Attributes

- interceding
- mediating
- protecting
- providing
- redeeming
- ruling

SING THE SONG

Learn about Melchizedek in Genesis 14:18–20 and Hebrews 5:5–6; 7:1–28.

Psalm

✺ 111 ✺

Holy and Awesome Is His Name

THEME

God works powerfully in the lives of his people, and those who embrace his ways are blessed.

HARMONY

Psalm 111 was composed to celebrate God's greatness and the privileges that come to those who belong to him. Such songs, called "praise psalms" and "thanksgiving psalms," were sung when Israel gathered for public worship.

SINGING IN TUNE

God is worthy of praise and thanksgiving for all he does in the lives of his people. Both his character and his works are majestic (v. 3), memorable (v. 4), enduring (v. 5), trustworthy (v. 7), and eternal (v. 8). God in his gracious kindness provides daily needs (v. 5), fulfills his promises (v. 6), and redeems from every form of evil (v. 9). Those who first sang this song thought back to God's delivering them from slavery in Egypt and then bringing them into the Promised Land (v. 6). Despite their many failures, God remained faithful to provide and protect, never wavering in his commitment to care for them. Those who are wise recognize the hand of God in the world and in their own lives, and they delight to live under his lordship, which is what it means to "fear" the Lord (v. 10).

MUSICAL NOTES

God's Grace

God "sent redemption to his people" (v. 9). God was faithful to call a people, Israel, and raise them up, providing and protecting them for a greater plan and purpose—gathering together a people to love through the redeeming work of his Son. The death of Christ on the cross and his resurrection from the dead have brought all God's people into the eternal Promised Land, which is life in the Lord's presence and his many blessings forever.

God's Attributes

- awesome
- faithful
- gracious
- holy
- righteous
- saving
- trustworthy

SING THE SONG

Describe how Colossians 1:3–14 is foreshadowed in Psalm 111.

Psalm

~⁓ 112 ⁓~

Well-Being for the Godly

THEME

Those who live for the Lord are blessed both materially and spiritually.

HARMONY

Psalm 112 has lots of similarity to the teaching and wording of the Bible's Wisdom Literature, primarily the book of Proverbs. The psalms that mirror the Bible's wisdom teaching are called "wisdom psalms."

SINGING IN TUNE

Praise flows easily from those committed to walking in God's ways, because they know the delight of those ways (v. 1). The blessings of living in the Lord touch every aspect of life, from family and provision of practical needs to growth in righteous character (vv. 2–3). Living near to God is also how guidance comes. As God's people immerse themselves in his Word, they develop discernment to govern their decisions and plans (v. 4). Those who know God best are those who trust him most, and this in turn produces a generous spirit. When we are confident of the Lord's provision, we don't feel anxiety about parting with our money or time but freely pour it out on behalf of others (vv. 5–9). The blessings of life in God are evident to everyone, and it provokes envy in those who reject him. But rather than turn to the Lord to find those blessings for themselves, they try to overcome their envy by destroying the godly; even so, they will not succeed (v. 10).

MUSICAL NOTES

God's Grace

In Psalm 112 the light that dawns in the darkness has to do with guidance—the kind that takes God's people deeper into God's ways. Today we have a fuller understanding of this light, which shines not outside of us but within our very own hearts. This light is a person, Jesus Christ, the one who said, "I am the light of the world. Whoever follows me will not walk in darkness, but will have the light of life" (John 8:12).

God's Attributes

- gracious
- guiding
- merciful
- trustworthy

SING THE SONG

Reflect on how John 12:46; Romans 13:12; 2 Corinthians 4:6; 6:14; and 1 John 2:8–9 enrich your understanding of Psalm 112 and help you understand how to apply it.

Psalm

~~~ 113 ~~~

Out of the Ash Heap

THEME

The great and powerful Lord takes note of the poor and needy and provides for them.

HARMONY

Psalm 113 was composed as a song of praise. It is included in the psalm collection that became known as the "Egyptian Hallel" (Psalms 113–118). These songs were sung at certain festivals during the year, and it is likely that the song Jesus and his disciples sang after the Passover meal (Matt. 26:30) came from this collection.

SINGING IN TUNE

God is worthy of ceaseless praise, and the psalmist calls everyone to participate (vv. 1–3). But this is no formal religious duty—it springs easily from the hearts of those who know God. The God who controls the world he made is able to provide for his creation (vv. 4–6). God takes special note of the helpless, meeting their needs and healing their heartbreak (vv. 7–9).

MUSICAL NOTES

God's Grace

Although God is high and mighty above his creation, he is never far away from anyone who calls on him. Because he is so powerful, he is able to take note of even the smallest details of our lives and do something about them, and in his compassion, that's exactly what he does. He knows what we need before we ask him, and he goes ahead of us to provide it. We see this most fully in the provision of his Son, whom he sent to save us from our sin and unite us to him forever. "He who did not spare his own Son but gave him up for us all, how will he not also with him graciously give us all things?" (Rom. 8:32).

God's Attributes

- compassionate
- giving
- kind
- majestic
- providing

SING THE SONG

Read the story of Hannah and how God provided for her, in 1 Samuel 1–2. Note where you find overlap with Psalm 113.

Psalm

114

Tremble, O Earth!

THEME

God has proven himself faithful in times past, so he can be trusted to care for his people in the present and in the future too.

HARMONY

Psalm 114 is a song of praise. God's people sang it together to celebrate their special role in God's worldwide plans. It is included in the psalm collection that became known as the "Egyptian Hallel." These songs were sung at certain festivals during the year, and it is likely that the song Jesus and his disciples sang after the Passover meal (Matt. 26:30) came from this collection.

SINGING IN TUNE

God is able to move heaven and earth (literally!) on behalf of his people. He controls his creation every moment, and for that reason, we have nothing to fear. When stressful circumstances come upon us, we can recall God's powerful work in times past, and because he is always faithful, we can be sure he will be no less faithful in the future. That's what the psalmist does. He recalls how God delivered his people from slavery in Egypt by parting the sea (vv. 1, 3). Afterward, when they were wandering in the desert, he provided all their daily needs, preserving them with water and drink in the rugged wilderness (vv. 4, 6, 8). In time, he fulfilled his promise and led them miraculously into the Promised Land (v. 5).

MUSICAL NOTES

God's Grace

To quench the thirst of his people in the desert, God turned a rock into a pool of water (v. 8), and from the apostle Paul we learn that this rock was Christ himself: "They drank from the spiritual Rock that followed them, and the Rock was Christ" (1 Cor. 10:4). Christ was there providing for his people even then, before he came to earth as a man. There has never been a time when God's provision for his people has not come through Christ. He was with Israel in the wilderness of the desert, and he is always with us in the deserts of our lives as well. Jesus is our rock—our strength—and the quencher of our thirst. Through him, God provides for every need of every one of his people.

God's Attributes

- creating
- delivering
- providing
- ruling

SING THE SONG

Read about God's miraculous provision for his people, in Exodus 14:1–31; 17:1–7 and Joshua 3:7–17.

Psalm

⋙ 115 ⋘

God Alone Is Lord

THEME

The Lord God alone is worthy of our trust and worship.

HARMONY

Psalm 115 was composed to encourage confident trust in God. It is included in the psalm collection that became known as the "Egyptian Hallel." These songs were sung at certain festivals during the year, and it is likely that the song Jesus and his disciples sang after the Passover meal (Matt. 26:30) came from this collection.

SINGING IN TUNE

The false god that we are most tempted to worship is our very own self, which the psalmist indicates at the beginning of his song: "Not to us, O LORD, not to us, but to your name give glory" (v. 1). Unbelievers might deny the one true God, but that doesn't make him any less God (vv. 2–3). Idol worship blinds the worshipers to the reality of God, even though the idols have no real power to do anything (vv. 4–7), and people who bow down to them become as senseless as the idols themselves (v. 8). In contrast to worthless idols, God is the help of his people. He is not only able but also willing to help them in every trouble and provide for their every need, and for that reason, he is the only one to trust (vv. 9–11).

MUSICAL NOTES

God's Grace

Self-sufficiency hides from us our dependence on the Lord. We are at all times and every moment utterly dependent on him for all things. For that reason, God in his grace is faithful to kick the lie of self-sufficiency out from under us so that we can live in joyful trust, resting in his ordering of our lives and circumstances. Life feels out of control because it is, so far as we are concerned. God is in control, and he exercises his control with love, mercy, and compassion.

God's Attributes

- reliable
- sovereign
- trustworthy

SING THE SONG

Explain what Isaiah 44:9–20 adds to your understanding of idols as they are described in Psalm 115.

Psalm

❧ 116 ❧

The Love of God

THEME

The psalmist expresses gratitude for the ways in which the Lord has personally cared for him.

HARMONY

Although Psalm 116 is a personal song of thanksgiving, it was composed for singing during public worship. It is included in the psalm collection that became known as the "Egyptian Hallel." These songs were sung at certain festivals during the year, and it is likely that the song Jesus and his disciples sang after the Passover meal (Matt. 26:30) came from this collection.

SINGING IN TUNE

God doesn't force people to love him; he demonstrates his own love for them in countless ways, so they cannot help but love him in return (vv. 1–2). No matter how dire our circumstances, we can call on God for rescue and be confident that he hears and delivers (vv. 3–9). The psalmist is so filled with love and gratitude that he ponders how to show his thanks to God in very public ways (vv. 12–14, 17–19). God takes note of and determines the daily life of his people; he also attends to the details of their death. Nothing about us slips past God's tender oversight (v. 15). The psalmist reaffirms his commitment to God and declares the joy he finds in serving the One who frees him from every form of tyranny.

MUSICAL NOTES

God's Grace

We owe God gratitude and love just because he's God—the holy, righteous Creator. Nevertheless, like a lover he woos his people. He could demand our love, but he doesn't, because true love is freely given. The one who loves gives himself to the one loved unreservedly. Love like this—God's love for his people—is portrayed as a marriage, which we see in the story of the prophet Hosea (chaps. 1–3). The New Testament also paints a picture of Christians as Christ's bride (see Eph. 5:25–33). That a holy God woos a sinful people is the epitome of grace. "In this is love, not that we have loved God but that he loved us and sent his Son to be the propitiation for our sins" (1 John 4:10).

God's Attributes
- faithful
- keeping
- listening
- loving
- protecting
- saving
- tender

SING THE SONG

Describe the ways in which Paul's story in 2 Corinthians 4:7–18 contains echoes of Psalm 116.

Psalm

☙ 117 ❧

God's Enduring Faithfulness

THEME

All people are invited to praise God for his love and faithfulness.

HARMONY

Psalm 117 was composed as a song of praise. Psalms of praise and thanksgiving celebrating God's greatness were sung when Israel gathered for public worship. It is included in the psalm collection that became known as the "Egyptian Hallel." These songs were sung at certain festivals during the year, and it is likely that the song Jesus and his disciples sang after the Passover meal (Matt. 26:30) came from this collection.

SINGING IN TUNE

In just two short verses, the psalmist issues a call to praise God. His invitation goes not only to God's own people but to all people everywhere, and that's because God's love isn't limited to just a select few. Only the people of God experience his special covenant blessings—steadfast love and faithfulness in every situation—but outsiders are invited to enter into God's fellowship and experience those blessings also. This short song helps God's people praise him, but it also points to their calling as God's ambassadors. God set apart Israel as those on whom he lavished his special affection, but it was never meant to stop with them. Through them, God began what he continues even today—calling people from every background to come into his eternal family.

MUSICAL NOTES

God's Grace

Through Israel God intended to call unbelievers to himself. That same call was issued later by Jesus, who instructed his disciples, "Go . . . and make disciples of all nations, baptizing them in the name of the Father and of the Son and of the Holy Spirit, teaching them to observe all that I have commanded you" (Matt. 28:19–20). God doesn't need the help of his people to build his kingdom; he grants them the privilege of participating in his work. With or without us, God's mission is sure because it was secured in Christ, who "ransomed people for God from every tribe and language and people and nation, and you have made them a kingdom and priests to our God, and they shall reign on the earth" (Rev. 5:9–10).

God's Attributes

- faithful
- loving
- sovereign

SING THE SONG

Read Romans 15:8–13 and explain why Christ is the only One who could fulfill God's call to bring in the lost.

Psalm

〜 118 〜

God's Enduring Love

THEME

God's love for his people will never cease.

HARMONY

Psalm 118 is another psalm of thanksgiving that believers gathered together to sing in celebration of God's greatness. It is included in the psalm collection that became known as the "Egyptian Hallel." These songs were sung at certain festivals during the year, and it is likely that the song Jesus and his disciples sang after the Passover meal (Matt. 26:30) came from this collection.

SINGING IN TUNE

Even when God's people cannot see evidence of his love, they can be sure it covers them, and declaring it repeatedly keeps them mindful of it (vv. 1–4). After a call to all Israel to remember God's love, the song takes on a personal note, as the psalmist recounts how the Lord delivered him from distress. He has learned that he has no reason to fear what people can do to hurt him, because God won't let plots against him succeed. He has also learned that trusting the Lord is a much wiser course than anxiously grabbing on to man-made solutions (vv. 5–13). Through his difficulties, which serve as the Lord's loving means of discipline, the psalmist has found strength to conquer his trouble and joy to fill his heart, and from this trusting perspective he is confident and secure (vv. 14–18). The song ends with all the people declaring the love of God in the sanctuary of God's house (vv. 19–29).

MUSICAL NOTES
God's Grace
The psalmist sang of Israel as a rejected stone (v. 22) because the surrounding nations scorned them. But Jesus suffered the most painful rejection of all. "He was despised and rejected by men, a man of sorrows and acquainted with grief; and as one from whom men hide their faces he was despised, and we esteemed him not" (Isa. 53:3). He willingly suffered the pain of rejection in order to become our cornerstone, and God accepts forever those who rest on his foundation.

God's Attributes
- defending
- good
- joy-giving
- loving
- protecting
- saving

SING THE SONG
From Ephesians 2:11–22, explain the importance of Jesus as our cornerstone.

Psalm

❧ 119 ❧

The Gift of God's Word

THEME

God's Word reveals the path to a blessed life.

HARMONY

Psalm 119 was composed to celebrate God's written Word. The composer cleverly wrote the song in what's called an "acrostic pattern," which means that a different letter of the Hebrew alphabet characterizes each stanza—twenty-two stanzas and twenty-two Hebrews letters.

SINGING IN TUNE

Experiencing the blessings of life with God is possible because God has revealed how—we direct our lives according to the pattern set forth in his written revelation, which the psalmist refers to as "law," "testimonies," "precepts," "statutes," "commandments," "rules," and "words." If we want to be shaped by God's Word, we must allow it to occupy our entire being, which the psalmist describes as walking, seeking, keeping, meditating on, delighting in, and clinging to. It also involves humility and prayer and personal commitment. An important aspect of God-centered living emerges in the psalm—wholeheartedness (vv. 2, 10, 34, 69, 145). Immersion in God's Word provides wisdom for daily life and the right perspective in times of suffering. The psalmist knows that walking in God's Word is the key to life, but he also knows his weakness and sin, which tempt him to turn elsewhere for blessing (v. 176).

God's Word is God's gift to his people, but we are totally dependent on the giver to live by it.

MUSICAL NOTES

God's Grace

God's written Word, the Bible, is God's greatest earthly gift to his people, second only to the living Word, Jesus. And because the living Word perfectly lived out the written Word, we are blessed beyond measure. Jesus fulfilled every precept found in Psalm 119, keeping the principles and commandments of this psalm, and he did so on our behalf. Our failure to live wholeheartedly is covered by Jesus, who lived it perfectly for us. Ultimately, he is Psalm 119 in human form, the Word that became flesh and dwelt among us (John 1:14).

God's Attributes

- providing
- revealing
- saving
- winsome
- wise

SING THE SONG

An undivided heart is a prerequisite for pursuing the life outlined in Psalm 119. Explain why, according to James 1:5–8; 4:1–10, wholeheartedness is so vital.

Psalm

❧ 120 ❧

A Song for the Lonely

THEME

God provides his presence and peace to those who seek him.

HARMONY

Psalms 120–134 are called Songs of Ascent, which means they were likely sung as God's people went up to Jerusalem to participate in sacred festivals and special times of worship. Psalm 120 was composed as a lament.

SINGING IN TUNE

Far away from the believing community, the psalmist is lonely, so he turns to the Lord for comfort. As he does, he calls to mind God's deliverance in times past (v. 1), which encourages him to trust God for deliverance in the present. The psalmist is somewhere he does not want to be, among people who promote dishonesty, disharmony, and destruction (vv. 3–7). Clearly he is homesick for the company of God's people back home in God's place, Jerusalem. Despite his lonely circumstances, he trusts that God is faithful and that God's ways of peace will ultimately prevail.

MUSICAL NOTES

God's Grace

We tend to identify ourselves with the psalmist, but apart from Christ we are actually more aligned with those who troubled him. We were "separated from Christ, alienated from the commonwealth of Israel and strangers to the covenants of promise, having no hope and without God in the world. But now in Christ Jesus you who once were far off have been brought near by the blood of Christ" (Eph. 2:12–13). The price of our peace was the cross—the greatest act of hostility the world has ever known. Yet God used it to destroy the barriers of hostility erected by sin and to restore the relationships that sin breaks, most especially with God himself.

God's Attributes

- faithful
- listening
- peaceful

SING THE SONG

Describe how Ephesians 2:11–22 shows the ultimate answer to the psalmist's prayer.

Psalm

❧ 121 ☙

God Our Helper

THEME

The Lord keeps watch over his people day and night and protects them in all they do.

HARMONY

Psalms 120–134 are called Songs of Ascent, which means they were likely sung as God's people went up to Jerusalem to participate in sacred festivals and special times of worship. Psalm 121 was composed to encourage trust in the Lord.

SINGING IN TUNE

The journey to Jerusalem could be long and frequently dangerous, and the psalmist, pondering the path ahead, recognizes his need for divine aid. Perhaps the hills he sees in the distance were those marking his destination, Jerusalem; or they might have been the hills on which people worshiped idols. In either case, he is on a journey, and he knows he cannot get where he is going under his own strength. The God who created the path must guard his people as they travel on it (vv. 1–2). They are set on reaching the place of God's special presence, and the psalmist is confident that they will get there because of God's watchful care. The travelers need sleep, but God does not, and he will protect them during the dark nights (vv. 3–4). The heat of the desert day won't harm them either, because God provides every necessity for completing the journey

268

(vv. 5–6). God's provision isn't merely physical; he also guards them from every evil snare that could derail their course (v. 7). God is with them not only as they journey but also when they get there. His care is constant (v. 8).

MUSICAL NOTES

God's Grace

Determined commitment propels our path, but reaching the destination is possible only because God gets us there. Left to ourselves, we would wander off course or be taken away. Determination simply isn't enough; Christ is our surety, and in him we are secure till the end. "Now to him who is able to keep you from stumbling and to present you blameless before the presence of his glory with great joy, to the only God, our Savior, through Jesus Christ our Lord, be glory, majesty, dominion, and authority, before all time and now and forever. Amen" (Jude 24–25).

God's Attributes

- creating
- helping
- keeping
- protecting
- saving

SING THE SONG

Consider how Paul's prayer in Ephesians 3:14–21 enables you to apply Psalm 121 to your own life.

Psalm

❦ 122 ❦

Gathered Together

THEME

Gathering together to worship God is a blessing and a privilege.

HARMONY

Psalms 120–134 are called Songs of Ascent, which means they were likely sung as God's people went up to Jerusalem to participate in sacred festivals and special times of worship. David composed Psalm 122 to celebrate Jerusalem, God's special city.

SINGING IN TUNE

An invitation to gather with others to worship God brought joy to David (vv. 1–2), and in gladness of heart he sings the blessings of belonging to the community of believers. In his day, that meant life in the city of Jerusalem, the special place where God revealed his presence, protection, and power to his people, and where the king governed the people in God's ways (vv. 3–5). Those who belonged to this covenant community were well aware of their privileges, so they prayed for the continuation of the blessings (vv. 6–8), and they dedicated themselves to pursue the welfare of this city (v. 9).

MUSICAL NOTES

God's Grace

God's people rejoiced in the king because he was the channel of God's blessings. Yet as far as kings go, David and his descendants failed to fulfill their God-appointed calling. Down through the years, God's ways were not upheld, and all the people suffered as a result. Nevertheless, their rejoicing wasn't in vain—it just went beyond what they could see. The rejoicing continues today because the perfect King has come, and his rule extends far beyond the walls of Jerusalem; by means of his Spirit, it's within the hearts of all who bow to him.

God's Attributes

- joy-giving
- protecting
- ruling

SING THE SONG

Consider how Ephesians 1:15–23 reveals the fulfillment of Psalm 121.

Psalm

ᕧ 123 ᕤ

Watching for Mercy

THEME

Those scorned by man find help and comfort in God's mercy.

HARMONY

Psalms 120–134 are called Songs of Ascent, which means they were likely sung as God's people went up to Jerusalem to participate in sacred festivals and special times of worship. Psalm 123 was composed as a lament.

SINGING IN TUNE

As God's people journey to Jerusalem, their joy is dampened by proud people who mock their faithfulness and hold them in contempt (v. 4). Pride and mockery go hand in hand. Feeling oppressed, the psalmist turns to God and waits expectantly for his help (v. 2). He does so because he is humble, and humility and a willingness to wait also go hand in hand. The attitude of the psalmist is that of a servant who stands ready to respond when a word of guidance or instruction is given. He is waiting for a sign of God's mercy, his favor, which, in this case, will include deliverance from the soul-crushing contempt aimed at the faithful.

MUSICAL NOTES

God's Grace

God delights to show mercy to those who call upon him, humbling themselves under his mighty hand. No matter how dire our circumstances, we can be confident of his merciful involvement if we have taken refuge in his Son, whom God sent to redeem us from sin and the wrath that stood against us. Those who are covered by Christ's atoning work on the cross, God's greatest act of mercy, can be confident of receiving mercy in all the little day-to-day ways it's needed. "Let us then with confidence draw near to the throne of grace, that we may receive mercy and find grace to help in time of need" (Heb. 4:16).

God's Attributes

- merciful
- saving

SING THE SONG

Consider how 1 Peter 5:5–11 equips you to apply Psalm 123.

Psalm

～～ 124 ～～

God Sides with His People

THEME

God is on the side of his people and comes to their rescue.

HARMONY

Psalms 120–134 are called Songs of Ascent, which means they were likely sung as God's people went up to Jerusalem to participate in sacred festivals and special times of worship. David composed Psalm 124 as a song of thanksgiving.

SINGING IN TUNE

Psalm 123 looked forward to deliverance, whereas Psalm 124 looks back on it. God's people have come through a crisis and been delivered from difficulty, and they attribute their deliverance solely to God. Were it not for the Lord's intervention, they would not have survived (vv. 1–5). Sometimes God's deliverances come early, just as trouble begins. Other times he waits until we are trapped (v. 7). In either case, God delivers, and he can be trusted with the when and the how.

MUSICAL NOTES

God's Grace

The Lord is *for* his people; he is on their side. Therefore, "if God is for us, who can be against us? He who did not spare his own Son but gave him up for us all, how will he not also with him graciously give us all things? Who shall bring any charge against God's elect? It is God who justifies. Who is to condemn? Christ Jesus is the one who died—more than that, who was raised—who is at the right hand of God, who indeed is interceding for us" (Rom. 8:31–34).

God's Attributes

- creating
- delivering
- helping
- ruling

SING THE SONG

Describe how Romans 8:26–30 builds on the portrayal of God in Psalm 124.

Psalm

❦ 125 ❧

Surrounded by God

THEME

God sees to it that those who are truly his people will never fall away from him.

HARMONY

Psalms 120–134 are called Songs of Ascent, which means they were likely sung as God's people went up to Jerusalem to participate in sacred festivals and special times of worship. Psalm 125 was composed to encourage faithfulness.

SINGING IN TUNE

As Jerusalem is sheltered all around by mountains, God surrounds his people; they are guarded within the circle of his protection, no matter the threats from without or within. King David and his descendants were called to lead God's people in God's good paths, but not all Israel's kings lived up to this divinely appointed calling. Therefore, there was always the risk that unfaithful kings could lead the people astray; but God controls even this (vv. 1–3). God blesses those who seek him, who desire to walk in his ways and in his fellowship, but those who refuse him, who desire autonomy from God, will eventually get what they wish for (vv. 4–5).

MUSICAL NOTES

God's Grace

The destiny of God's true followers, those united to him in Christ, is guaranteed. They will never fall away because God has promised to keep them, and he secured his promise when he sent his Son to redeem them. We are safe in the care of the One who claimed, "I give them eternal life, and they will never perish, and no one will snatch them out of my hand. My Father, who has given them to me, is greater than all, and no one is able to snatch them out of the Father's hand. I and the Father are one" (John 10:28–30).

God's Attributes

- defending
- just
- protecting

SING THE SONG

Describe how Jesus's prayer in John 17:1–26 fulfills the promise of Psalm 125.

Psalm

❧ 126 ❧

Reaping Joy

THEME

God's faithfulness in times past supplies his people with confident hope for the future.

HARMONY

Psalms 120–134 are called Songs of Ascent, which means they were likely sung as God's people went up to Jerusalem to participate in sacred festivals and special times of worship. Psalm 126 was composed as a lament.

SINGING IN TUNE

In contrast to the unstable, often fleeting deliverances we achieve for ourselves, God's deliverances are sure and permanent, and they are accompanied by a happiness we can never simply produce. That's been true of God's people in every age, as the psalmist shows us (vv. 1–3). In this life, new trials come, and fresh deliverances are regularly needed, but God's faithfulness in the past assures his people of help in every difficulty (v. 4). We can walk with him in trust and obedience even in grievous circumstances, because the outcome is sure (vv. 5–6). "Now to him who is able to do far more abundantly than all that we ask or think, according to the power at work within us, to him be glory in the church and in Christ Jesus throughout all generations, forever and ever. Amen" (Eph. 3:20–21).

MUSICAL NOTES

God's Grace

Our God restores rather than destroys, and his restorative work—in the world and in our own lives—always exceeds our expectations. God restores us to himself through the work of Christ on the cross, but that is just the beginning of a whole restorative process. Once we are in Christ, God's restorative work becomes transformative as he works in us by his Spirit to conform us to the image of Christ. One day, that transformation will be complete, and we will enjoy God's fellowship in the new Jerusalem, the restored world. In Christ, the best is always yet to come.

God's Attributes

- joy-giving
- provider
- restoring

SING THE SONG

Describe the ways in which Romans 8:18–25 shows the fulfillment of Psalm 126.

Psalm

~~ 127 ~~

Prosperity Depends on the Lord

THEME

Wise planning and diligent effort are vital, but success in any endeavor depends solely on God.

HARMONY

Psalms 120–134 are called Songs of Ascent, which means they were likely sung as God's people went up to Jerusalem to participate in sacred festivals and special times of worship. Psalm 127 was composed by Solomon and has lots of similarity to the teaching and wording of the Bible's Wisdom Literature, primarily the book of Proverbs.

SINGING IN TUNE

The path of God's Word leads away from self-sufficiency to dependence on the Lord, yet nowhere in Scripture are we told to "let go and let God." Depending on God is no call to passivity; to the contrary, the wisdom of Solomon calls us to be proactive in living out our callings and performing our daily tasks. So the work is ours; however, the success of our work is not. The outcome of all we do lies completely in the hands of God (v. 1). That's why the desire to control is a root of so much of our anxiety—control is only an illusion. Dependence on God involves getting up in the morning and performing our duties to the best of our abilities and then, at the end of the day, leaving all we've said and done in God's hands and going to sleep (v. 2). As the song progresses, Solomon shifts his tune to the blessings of family life (vv. 3–5), yet his point is the same—our family and its growth are not our own doing. Everything we have and all we do thrives only through the Lord's blessing.

MUSICAL NOTES

God's Grace

How much energy and time we waste on anxious care! Do we trust the Lord? He who numbers every hair on our head (Matt. 10:30) is actively involved in our lives—our family, our job, our education, where we live, our health, and all we do. Often our anxiety springs not from doubting God's power to know and do what's best but from a demand that he do what *we* deem best. We can let go of that, because he always works everything for our good in Christ (Rom. 8:28).

God's Attributes

- protecting
- providing
- sovereign

SING THE SONG

Explain how John 15:1–5 provides application for Psalm 127.

Psalm

~~~ 128 ~~~

Walking the Path of Blessing

THEME

Following the Lord and walking in his ways lead to blessing.

HARMONY

Psalms 120–134 are called Songs of Ascent, which means they were likely sung as God's people went up to Jerusalem to participate in sacred festivals and special times of worship. Psalm 128 was composed as a wisdom psalm.

SINGING IN TUNE

Everyone who walks in God's ways finds blessing and well-being (vv. 1–2). That's the teaching of the Bible's Wisdom Books, such as Proverbs, which explains why Psalm 128 is called a "wisdom psalm." The psalmist illustrates his lesson with the head of a household. A man who leads his home according to God's Word creates an environment in which his family thrives (vv. 3–4), and he centers his life in Jerusalem, the special city where God blessed his people with his presence, protection, and provision (vv. 5–6). Believers today don't need to go to Jerusalem to enjoy God; they find these same blessings in the family of God's people, the church.

MUSICAL NOTES

God's Grace

As our Creator, God doesn't owe us anything; it is we who owe him a debt we could never pay. Yet God takes pleasure in pouring out blessing on his people. He wants us to discover that walking in his ways not only pleases him but also conduces to our happiness—he has designed us to find delight in what he delights in. "Every good gift and every perfect gift is from above, coming down from the Father of lights, with whom there is no variation or shadow due to change" (James 1:17).

God's Attributes

- peace-giving
- prospering
- righteous

SING THE SONG

Describe what Proverbs 3:1–27 adds to your understanding of Psalm 128.

Psalm

✣✣ 129 ✣✣

Righteousness Prevails

THEME

God allows affliction in the lives of his people, but he is always faithful to deliver them.

HARMONY

Psalms 120–134 are called Songs of Ascent, which means they were likely sung as God's people went up to Jerusalem to participate in sacred festivals and special times of worship. Those who sang Psalm 129 found encouragement to trust God as they traveled.

SINGING IN TUNE

It seems counterintuitive, but in God's economy, suffering leads to song. The apostle Paul explains how: "We rejoice in our sufferings, knowing that suffering produces endurance, and endurance produces charac-ter, and character produces hope, and hope does not put us to shame, because God's love has been poured into our hearts through the Holy Spirit who has been given to us" (Rom. 5:3–5). That's what the psalm-ist is singing about in Psalm 129. The people of Israel were persecuted for their faith, and their suffering left deep scars, yet their persecutors didn't get the last word because God cut them off. Righteousness in-evitably triumphs over evil because God himself is righteous (vv. 1–4); that's why God is honored when his people pray that evildoers will experience shame (vv. 5–8).

MUSICAL NOTES

God's Grace

The suffering of Christ on the cross guarantees hope as the fruit of suffering for all those united to him by faith. "Surely he has borne our griefs and carried our sorrows. . . . He was wounded for our transgressions; he was crushed for our iniquities; upon him was the chastisement that brought us peace, and with his wounds we are healed" (Isa. 53:4–5).

God's Attributes

- delivering
- hope-giving
- just
- righteous

SING THE SONG

Describe how Paul's experience of suffering in 2 Corinthians 4:7–18 echoes the experience of God's people in Psalm 129.

Psalm

∼≫ 130 ≪∼

Mercy

THEME

God shows mercy to repentant sinners.

HARMONY

Psalms 120–134 are called Songs of Ascent, which means they were likely sung as God's people went up to Jerusalem to participate in sacred festivals and special times of worship. Psalm 130 was composed as a lament for sin.

SINGING IN TUNE

God lifts us up, but sin takes us down. That's why the psalmist prays from the depths—he has fallen down into sin (vv. 1–2). He wants what he so desperately needs—God's mercy. His pleas contain no excuses or resolve to do better in the future. He bases his case solely on God's mercy (vv. 3–4). For that reason, the psalmist has confidence. Our determination to do good is fickle, and so often we know it; only God keeps his promises, one of which is to forgive. The psalmist's honesty about his sin and his plea for mercy leave him filled with anticipation of the restoration and renewal God will work in his heart and life (vv. 5–6), and he encourages the whole believing community to follow his path of repentance (vv. 7–8).

MUSICAL NOTES

God's Grace

If the Lord were to "mark iniquities" (v. 3), none of us would have hope. We would be left in the muck and destruction of our sin. But God doesn't merely sweep our sins under the rug out of his sight; every sin must be paid for. Because God is holy, he must "mark" iniquity. But we don't get the mark for ours, because God marked Jesus instead. All our sin was placed on him when he went to the cross. Jesus is our confidence before God, the basis of our plea for mercy. "Let us then with confidence draw near to the throne of grace, that we may receive mercy and find grace to help in time of need" (Heb. 4:16).

God's Attributes

- forgiving
- merciful
- redeeming
- restoring

SING THE SONG

Make application of Psalm 130 from Titus 2:11–14.

Psalm

❧ 131 ❧

A Picture of Humility

THEME

Humility breeds trust in God and stability in our walk of faith.

HARMONY

Psalms 120–134 are called Songs of Ascent, which means they were likely sung as God's people went up to Jerusalem to participate in sacred festivals and special times of worship. David composed Psalm 131 as a song of confidence.

SINGING IN TUNE

Only the humble enjoy fellowship with God and experience his peace. David, Israel's great king, understood this. He didn't rely on his high position for favor or believe that his powerful earthly calling made him spiritually superior (v. 1). Because he was humble, gaps in his understanding didn't undo him. Such is the case for anyone, including those in authority—whether bosses or parents or kings like David—when humility rules the heart. A humble heart relies on God's knowledge and wisdom and doesn't panic about personal limitations. David likens the state of his soul to a weaned child, one that can be in his mother's presence without anxious clamoring, and he has been an active participant in cultivating such humility: "I have calmed and quieted my soul" (v. 2). Finally, David calls all God's people to hope, because humility and hope go hand in hand (v. 3).

MUSICAL NOTES

God's Grace

A compulsion for knowledge and understanding is driven by a craving to control our lives and relationships. We fear that a lack of understanding—about God or the world—will leave us fragile and insecure. But it's actually the craving itself that weakens us. God can be trusted to run his world and every detail of our lives. Therefore, we can humble ourselves, forsaking the craving to control, by leaning on Jesus, who tells us, "Come to me, all who labor and are heavy laden, and I will give you rest. Take my yoke upon you, and learn from me, for I am gentle and lowly in heart, and you will find rest for your souls" (Matt. 11:28–29).

God's Attributes

- all-knowing
- all-powerful
- trustworthy

SING THE SONG

Consider how 1 Peter 5:6–10 enables you to apply Psalm 131.

Psalm

❧ 132 ❧

God Fulfills His Promises

THEME

God keeps his promises.

HARMONY

Psalms 120–134 are called Songs of Ascent, which means they were likely sung as God's people went up to Jerusalem to participate in sacred festivals and special times of worship. The background to Psalm 132 is found in 2 Samuel 7.

SINGING IN TUNE

As God's people journey toward God's house, the temple in Jerusalem, they reflect on the origin of this great blessing—God had placed in David's heart a longing to build a temple, a dwelling place for God (vv. 1–7). Although David was not the one to build it, his dream came true when his son Solomon undertook this great construction project. As the people make their pilgrimage to the temple, they rejoice that they will meet and worship God there. In the temple they will encounter God's commandments ("the ark of his might," v. 8) and the priests who will offer the sacrifices to atone for their sins. They are joyful about finding God's presence there and receiving the covenant blessings God had promised to provide (vv. 8–10). The people specifically recall God's promise that a descendant of David will always rule and protect them on God's behalf

(vv. 11–12). In God's presence, through his appointed king, God will provide both materially and spiritually for his people (vv. 13–18).

MUSICAL NOTES

God's Grace

Jesus Christ is the fulfillment of everything that Israel journeyed to enjoy. First, he is the temple in human flesh, the manifestation of God's presence to his people (John 2:18–22; Rev. 21:22). Second, he is the satisfying bread that God gives to the needy. "I am the bread of life," Jesus said; "whoever comes to me shall not hunger, and whoever believes in me shall never thirst" (John 6:35). Finally, as the Great High Priest, he doesn't need to be clothed with salvation; rather, his salvation clothes his people (Zech. 3:1–5; Rev. 7:9).

God's Attributes

- eternal
- faithful
- kingly
- redeeming
- saving

SING THE SONG

Consider how Acts 7:44–50; 1 Corinthians 3:16–17; Colossians 1:15–20; and Revelation 21:1–5 show the fuller meaning of Psalm 132.

Psalm

❧ 133 ☙

A Shared Life

THEME

God blesses his gathered people.

HARMONY

Psalms 120–134 are called Songs of Ascent, which means they were likely sung by those who went up to Jerusalem to participate in sacred festivals and special times of worship. Psalm 133 was composed by David to celebrate the unity of God's people.

SINGING IN TUNE

By God's design, unity brings joy (v. 1), most especially when God's people gather together for worship. Such unity strengthens faith and promotes holiness, which is what the psalmist means by "precious oil on the head . . . of Aaron" (v. 2). Aaron and his descendants served as the priests who mediated between God and his people (see Ex. 30:22–33). Unity also deepens trust, because as believers gather together to worship, they are reminded of all God is and has promised to be for his people in providing for their every need. Just as the dew from Mount Hermon flows down and waters the land beneath it (v. 3), God's people are dependent for their every need on what flows down from God's hand. Gathered together, the people praise and thank God for his blessings, and as they do, they are reminded afresh that he is the source of the life they share together.

MUSICAL NOTES

God's Grace

The blessings of unity fall on God's people in every age. Believers today don't need to travel to Jerusalem to enjoy it; we gather wherever we can, in local churches. Although each believer has a personal walk with God, the Christian life is not meant to be solitary. God's provision for his people in this life comes primarily through the united whole, of which each individual and every faithful local church is a part. Together, united to Christ, we are loved by God and experience the riches of his grace.

God's Attributes

- holy
- providing
- relational

SING THE SONG

Describe what Jesus's prayer for believers in John 17:20–26 adds to your understanding of Psalm 133.

Psalm

❧❧ 134 ❧❧

In God's House

THEME

God delights in both the praise of his people and their requests.

HARMONY

Psalms 120–134 are called Songs of Ascent, which means they were likely sung by those who went up to Jerusalem to participate in sacred festivals and special times of worship. Psalm 134 rejoices in actually being inside the temple and worshiping.

SINGING IN TUNE

This short psalm wraps up the Songs of Ascent with a final call to worship. All God's people are invited to participate, yet the psalmist directs his call most especially to those whose calling is to serve God in the temple (v. 1). Humble worshipers lift their hands not only in praise to God (v. 2) but also in supplication, as they seek his presence and provision. They emphasize Zion, Jerusalem, because that's where God chose to dwell with his people, and "he who made heaven and earth" provides for their needs (v. 3).

MUSICAL NOTES

God's Grace

God's holiness sets him high above his people, yet he welcomes their praise and prayers. From Psalm 134 we see that praise can be short and

simple; it's the heart of the worshiper that God cares about, not flowery language. A simple song, an upheld hand, and a quiet word—he hears and responds to each one that issues from a heart of faith.

God's Attributes

- creating
- holy
- praiseworthy

SING THE SONG

Note how Colossians 3:16–17 provides application for Psalm 134.

Psalm

❧ 135 ❧

Bless the Lord!

THEME

God showers every blessing on his people, which makes them the most privileged of any on earth.

HARMONY

Psalm 135 was composed in celebration of God's greatness and the privileges that come to those who belong to him. This praise song calls on all God's people to participate.

SINGING IN TUNE

Those who know God can't help but praise him. They have witnessed how good he is, most especially in choosing them to belong to him (vv. 1–4). God is worthy of praise because he controls the world, something only he can do because he created it (vv. 5–7). Nothing is outside the sphere of his sovereignty; he works in nature and in the hearts of human beings for the good of his people. Israel experienced God's mighty power when he brought them out of slavery in Egypt and gave them possession of the Promised Land (vv. 8–12). Nations and lands rise and fall, but God is unchanging. He has always been who he is—just and compassionate toward his people (vv. 13–14). Offering worship to anything or anyone else is folly, because only God can provide and deliver (vv. 15–18). Idols are worthless, and those who trust in them will, in time, become equally as worthless, because human beings are always conformed to what they worship. God alone is Lord, and he alone is worthy of praise (vv. 19–20).

MUSICAL NOTES

God's Grace

God is worthy of our exclusive praise and trust because he is the only One who can actually take care of us. Already he has provided through his Son what we most need—cleansing from the sin that separates us from him. In Christ, God is our kind Father, and "he who did not spare his own Son but gave him up for us all, how will he not also with him graciously give us all things?" (Rom. 8:32).

God's Attributes

- compassionate
- creating
- delivering
- good
- providing
- sovereign
- sustaining

SING THE SONG

Explain how Romans 8:28–39 reveals the fulfillment of Psalm 135.

Psalm

~~ 136 ~~

God's Steadfast Love

THEME

The love of God can be tangibly traced in his work down through history.

HARMONY

Psalm 136 is a song of thanksgiving. It is the only psalm to have the same refrain for every verse.

SINGING IN TUNE

The overarching theme behind everything God does is love—his steady, unfailing commitment to prosper his people in him. Love underlies his goodness and sovereignty (vv. 1–3), his creation of the world (vv. 4–9), and his deliverances of his people from trouble. In that regard, the singers call to mind Israel's miraculous deliverance from slavery in Egypt (vv. 10–16). God's love also assures that he will fulfill all his promises, as he did when he brought Israel into the Promised Land (vv. 17–22). God's love underlies his attentive care for the poor and needy and the justice he works out for the oppressed (vv. 23–25). God does nothing in creation or in our own lives that isn't governed by his love, and for that, he is worthy of ceaseless thanks (v. 26).

MUSICAL NOTES

God's Grace

God reveals his love for us in countless ways, big and small, every day, from the moment we awaken. His love underlies every good thing we have. His love also underlies every trial we experience. His love for us is never tinged with anger or irritation, not even when we sin. Of this we can be assured, "for God so loved the world, that he gave his only Son, that whoever believes in him should not perish but have eternal life. For God did not send his Son into the world to condemn the world, but in order that the world might be saved through him" (John 3:16–17).

God's Attributes
- faithful
- loving

SING THE SONG

Describe what Romans 8:38–39; 1 Corinthians 13:1–13; and 1 John 4:9–21 add to your understanding of God's love.

$\mathcal{P}\!\mathit{salm}$

❧❧❧ 137 ❦❦❦

When Singing Hurts

THEME

God disciplines his children and judges the unrepentant.

HARMONY

Psalm 137 was composed for the community to lament an extended season of suffering and to express a longing for righteousness to triumph over evil.

SINGING IN TUNE

The Babylonian invasion and captivity of God's people in 586 BC was no surprise. The prophets had been warning of it for years, calling God's people to stop seeking security in pagan nations and return to the trustworthy Lord. But the warning went unheeded, and eventually God's judgment fell. God's people were forcibly taken from the Land of Promise and carried off to Babylon, where they were no longer able to worship God freely. There they were cruelly mocked for their faith (vv. 2–3). Even in judgment, however, God meant to redeem, not destroy. The exile in Babylon was designed to bring about repentance in the hearts of his people and make them long for him afresh (v. 1). In time, they were allowed to return home, but the horrors of the exile haunted them for years to come, and they commit to never forget God and his ways again (vv. 4–6). Remembering the horrors, the people pray for justice, asking God to do to their enemies what was done to them (vv. 7–9). God does not invite prayers for revenge, but our takeaway from this psalm is that praying for the destruction of evil is good and right.

MUSICAL NOTES

God's Grace

When someone hurts us, even when our own sin is a contributing factor, our natural instinct is to make our tormenter feel the same pain in return. That instinct springs from the sin that, apart from Christ, characterizes all we feel and think. In union with him, however, our desires and the things we pray for are reshaped, because the Holy Spirit is at work to transform us to be like the One who suffered brutal, unjust treatment, without complaint, for our sakes.

God's Attributes

- fatherly
- just
- renewing
- restoring
- righteous

SING THE SONG

Meditate on 1 Peter 2:18–25.

Psalm

~~ 138 ~~

God Fulfills His Purposes for His People

THEME

God preserves his people and fulfills his purpose for each one.

HARMONY

David composed Psalm 138 as a song of thanksgiving. Although the thanks offered is personal, it was included in the Psalter for singing in public worship.

SINGING IN TUNE

David offers wholehearted thanks for the love and faithfulness God has shown him over the years. God has demonstrated time and again that in him alone are strength and security (vv. 1–3). One day, every authority on earth will bow before God, and all who embrace his word from the heart will turn to him with joy and thanksgiving (vv. 4–5). Coming to God requires humility, because God reveals himself only to the humble (v. 6). Those who come will enjoy all the blessings God showers on his people. Even so, a close walk with God is no guarantee that troubles won't come. But when they do, God brings his people through them and ensures that his purpose is fulfilled in the life of each one (vv. 7–8).

MUSICAL NOTES

God's Grace

God has a plan for the family of his people as a whole and for each individual within it. His overarching plan is to secure our salvation in Christ, transform us into Christ's likeness, and then bring us home to be with him forever in glory (Rom. 8:28–30). And to get us there—and others along with us—he has a special plan for how that will work out in each individual life. We don't always see his hand at work, but with the apostle Paul we can say, "I am sure of this, that he who began a good work in you will bring it to completion at the day of Jesus Christ" (Phil. 1:6).

God's Attributes

- compassionate
- holy
- loving
- powerful
- sovereign

SING THE SONG

Explain how Romans 12:1–2; 1 Thessalonians 4:1–8; 5:16–22; and 1 Peter 4:16–19 help you understand God's will for your life.

Psalm

~~~ 139 ~~~

Known and Loved

THEME

God knows his people intimately and cares for them individually.

HARMONY

Many of the psalms were sung in celebration of God's greatness and the privileges that come to those who belong to him. These praise songs were sung when Israel gathered for public worship. Psalm 139 was composed by David.

SINGING IN TUNE

In this intensely personal song, David sings in wonder about the extent of God's care. God knows everything about each one of his people. He knows what they do from the moment they awaken until they go to sleep at night, and in between he knows every thought they think and every word they say, even before it crosses their lips (vv. 1–4). But God doesn't just know his people; he also rules over the choices they make and the ventures they undertake (v. 5). His oversight of each and every life is beyond human comprehension (vv. 6, 17–18). No one can escape God's presence, his knowing eye and guiding hand. People can run, but God's love won't let them hide (vv. 7–12). God planned everything about us before we were born—our looks, our family, our talents and gifts, and all the circumstances in which these play out (vv. 13–16). Anyone who knows God and has experienced his intimate care develops an increasing hatred for evil, which is why David prays for an end to every form it takes (vv. 19–22). Finally, David wants nothing to hinder his walk with the Lord, so he asks for the light of God's righteousness to shine into his heart in order to recognize and then forsake any hindrance (vv. 23–24).

MUSICAL NOTES

God's Grace

That the Creator God of the universe would bother to care so personally for human beings is indeed beyond our comprehension. We do know that his attentiveness isn't due to our worthiness; it springs solely from his love and his determination to bless those he has called to himself through Christ. "God, being rich in mercy, because of the great love with which he loved us, even when we were dead in our trespasses, made us alive together with Christ—by grace you have been saved—and raised us up with him and seated us with him in the heavenly places in Christ Jesus, so that in the coming ages he might show the immeasurable riches of his grace in kindness toward us in Christ Jesus" (Eph. 2:4–7).

God's Attributes

- all-knowing
- guiding
- holy
- personal
- redeeming
- sovereign

SING THE SONG

Describe how Matthew 6:25–34 helps you trust God as he is portrayed in Psalm 139.

Psalm

❧ 140 ☙

Delivered from Evil

THEME

God is more powerful in the lives of his people than any evil that comes against them.

HARMONY

Psalm 140 is a song of lament composed by David. His song contains a prayer for the downfall of the wicked, but revenge isn't his motive. His hope is the triumph of righteousness over evil. For that reason, songs like Psalm 140 show us how to pray when evil threatens us.

SINGING IN TUNE

Pressing troubles produce urgent prayers, as we see with David, who begins his song with a plea for help. Ungodly men are seeking his downfall, plotting how to harm him, and the threat is clearly over-whelming (vv. 1–3). David is no match for his enemies; he needs the all-knowing, all-powerful Lord to foil their plot (vv. 4–5), and his trust is strengthened as he remembers God's faithful deliverances in times past (vv. 6–7). David prays not only that God will defend him but also that God will go on the offensive against his enemies, thwarting their evil desires and causing them to fall victim to their own schemes (vv. 8–11). David is well acquainted with God's ways, that he is just, so he is confident that God will sustain him until all danger has passed (vv. 12–13).

MUSICAL NOTES

God's Grace

Only some of us can relate to the life-threatening persecution David experienced, but we all share with him two common enemies—sin and Satan. Both seek to destroy us, and were it not for divine rescue, we'd have no chance of survival. But in Jesus, God defeated these enemies. Through Christ's death on the cross, God worked justice for his people and secured the defeat of sin and Satan for all who trust in his mercy. Therefore, when trials and temptations weigh us down, we can sing David's song because Jesus is the strength of our salvation and has covered our head in the day of battle (v. 7).

God's Attributes

- delivering
- guarding
- just
- saving

SING THE SONG

Describe how Psalm 140 together with Romans 3:9–26 shapes your understanding of both God and human beings.

Psalm

❧ 141 ❧

Love God and Hate Evil

THEME

Love for God and his ways leads to hatred of sin.

HARMONY

Psalm 141 is another song of lament composed by King David. Like many of his laments, this one arose from his personal problems, but it was meant for the whole community to sing and apply.

SINGING IN TUNE

David conveys a good bit of urgency as he petitions God about two primary concerns. First, he recognizes his need for God's help to refrain from sin, both with his words (v. 3) and in his affections. He has the humility to know his own weakness, how vulnerable he can be to temptation, most especially in the company of unbelievers (v. 4). David has the wisdom to recognize the value of godly companionship and the accountability for righteous living that accompanies it (v. 5). "Faithful are the wounds of a friend; profuse are the kisses of an enemy" (Prov. 27:6). The second part of David's song builds on the first: he prays directly against evil and those who seek to work it into his life (vv. 5–10). He recognizes how easily he can be snared, and he asks to be held back from those traps and that those who love sin will realize personally how destructive it is.

MUSICAL NOTES

God's Grace

David hates sin and is fearful of falling into it because he knows that walking with God and living in his ways is far more enjoyable than all the worldly delights of the wicked (v. 4). Only God's grace enables anyone to see the horror of sin and the blessedness of obedience, and he reveals it through Jesus. The giving of spiritual sight was the deeper miracle behind every blind eye Jesus opened while he walked this earth. Salvation in Christ doesn't mean we will never sin, but it does mean we will hate when we do.

God's Attributes

- delightful
- good
- protecting
- righteous
- saving

SING THE SONG

Deepen your understanding of Psalm 141 by meditating on 1 Corinthians 10:1–13; 15:33–34 and James 1:13–18.

Psalm

~~~ 142 ~~~

Known, Loved, and Delivered

THEME

God rescues those who cannot rescue themselves.

HARMONY

Psalm 142 is a song of lament composed by King David. The trouble he sings about is once again personal, but the whole community sang it, because their well-being was tied to that of the king. David wrote Psalm 142 while hiding from his rival Saul.

SINGING IN TUNE

On the run from his enemy Saul, David takes refuge in a cave. There, cut off from the comforts and security of home, he earnestly seeks both comfort and security in God himself (v. 1). A mark of David's faith is the way in which he freely pours out his trouble to God (v. 2). He knows that God welcomes and responds to prayers of raw honesty. Although David is overwhelmed by his circumstances, God is not (v. 3). There in the cave, David can see no way out, and he feels utterly alone (vv. 4, 6). Our most earnest prayers often arise from our most hopeless situations. With no human help at hand and no strategy to deploy, David is reminded that God is sufficient—more than enough— to meet his needs (vv. 5, 7).

MUSICAL NOTES

God's Grace

We won't trust God if we believe he demonstrates his love by preventing every crisis. To the contrary, God's love leads to caves. So long as we are surrounded by friends and a multitude of options, we don't fully lean on him, and only when we fully lean do we discover that he is everything he has promised to be. No matter our trouble, we can be confident of rescue, of receiving the mercy David pleaded for (v. 1), because of what God did in a different cave—the tomb of Jesus. The Son of God lay dead in that cave, but after three days he was brought out alive, and "God, being rich in mercy, because of the great love with which he loved us, even when we were dead in our trespasses, made us alive together with Christ . . . and raised us up with him . . . so that in the coming ages he might show the immeasurable riches of his grace in kindness toward us in Christ Jesus" (Eph. 2:4–7).

God's Attributes

- all-sufficient
- delivering
- giving
- listening
- merciful
- protecting

SING THE SONG

Consider how Luke 24 is the fulfillment of Psalm 142 and our guarantee of rescue from every cave.

$\mathcal{P}\!salm$

ᵛᵛ⁾⁾ 143 ᵛᵛᵛ

Safe on Level Ground

THEME

The psalmist trusts in God, not in himself, for safety and guidance.

HARMONY

Lament psalms sometimes include an acknowledgment of sin, and when they do, they are called "penitential psalms." Such is the case with Psalm 143. These prayerful songs were sung individually such as we see with David here, and they were also sung by those gathered together for worship. In either case, those singing have confidence because God is merciful and kind.

SINGING IN TUNE

Once again David finds himself in dire straits, circumstances that necessitate divine intervention (vv. 3–4). He pleads for God's help, and he bases his request not on the strength of his praying or his attempts to live righteously but on God's faithfulness (vv. 1–2). As David calls to mind God's faithfulness in times past, his longing for relief intensifies as does his yearning for God himself (vv. 5–7). Great suffering is meant to intensify our thirst for divine fellowship. Because David trusts God, he is eager to receive God's guidance, and he prays that his trouble will deepen his understanding of God's ways (vv. 8–10). Gained from focusing on God in his Word and through prayer is an accurate view of God, which David has as the psalm ends—he is confident that deliverance will come (v. 12).

MUSICAL NOTES

God's Grace

God's "good Spirit" (v. 10) led David, and he leads God's people today as well. When Jesus was raised from the dead and taken back into heaven, the Holy Spirit was sent to be our divine Helper and to lead us from the inside out (John 14:16, 26; 15:26; 16:7). The Spirit lives within us, transforming us to be like Christ, teaching us to pray, strengthening us where we are weak (Rom. 8:26–27), and preparing us for our eventual home in heaven.

God's Attributes

- delivering
- faithful
- guiding
- listening
- loving
- powerful
- teaching

SING THE SONG

Note all the ways in which Romans 8 depicts the work of the Holy Spirit in the lives of believers.

$\mathcal{P}_{\text{salm}}$

⟫⟫⟫ 144 ⟪⟪⟪

Finishing Well

THEME

Walking faithfully with God necessitates dependence on God.

HARMONY

David composed Psalm 144 as a royal psalm. These songs were designed to focus the believing community on the vital role that Israel's kings played in God's plan to provide for his people and, most of all, to celebrate God as the ultimate King.

SINGING IN TUNE

King David was appointed by God to lead the people in God's righteous ways, and in order to do so well, he must humbly rely on God's love and care (vv. 1–2). He knows that only God, the Creator of the world and everything in it, can enable him to fulfill his royal calling (vv. 3–8). He is dependent on God for victory on the battlefield and for prosperity in his homeland where he rules (vv. 9–14). The blessings that God gives David will then pour down on all the people (v. 15). David is sure of both God's character and his own calling, which is what enables him to pray with bold confidence for God's blessing on his kingly endeavors.

MUSICAL NOTES

God's Grace

We, too, have a divine calling—we have been called into the fellowship of God's Son, Jesus Christ our Lord (1 Cor. 1:9). As king of Israel, David prayed for God's protection. As King of kings, Jesus protects us. As king of Israel, David prayed for peace and prosperity. As King of kings, Jesus brings us peace and provides us with abundant life. Because serving this King is our calling, we can pray with the same boldness for God's blessing as we seek to live it out and be assured of victory.

God's Attributes

- creating
- delivering
- kingly
- providing

SING THE SONG

Describe how Colossians 3:1–24 provides a way to pray Psalm 144 personally.

$\mathcal{P}\mathit{salm}$

❧ 145 ☙

Our Generous God

THEME

God is generous and kind toward all his creatures, but he shows special favor to his own people.

HARMONY

Psalm 145, David's final song in the Psalter, was composed to praise the goodness of God.

SINGING IN TUNE

David thanks and praises God every day, because every moment of every day God showers his creation with love and kindness. David begins his praise with the character of God himself—specifically, God's greatness (vv. 1–3). To this he adds praise for God's majesty, goodness, righteousness, grace, mercy, patience, love, glory, kindness, sovereignty, and holiness. Arising from who God *is* are all the things God *does*. He intervenes to stop calamity and sin and raises up those who are falling under it (v. 14). He takes note of practical needs and provides them, knowing when and what to give in each circumstance to every person (v. 15). He goes beyond just meeting needs to also fulfilling desires (vv. 16, 19). He hears and responds to every cry directed to him (v. 18), and he safeguards his own righteousness and his relationship with his people (v. 20). God never acts in any way toward any creature contrary to what David sets forth in his song.

MUSICAL NOTES

God's Grace

"The LORD is righteous in all his ways and kind in all his works" (v. 17). That "all" is unconditional. Everything God plans for us, even the painful things, are rooted in what he knows is good and right, and our all-knowing, all-powerful God governs the details of each of our lives with pure kindness. So whatever he gives and takes away, provides or withholds, we can trust him absolutely. After all, "he who did not spare his own Son but gave him up for us all, how will he not also with him graciously give us all things?" (Rom. 8:32). God knows, even if we do not, that Jesus is the deepest desire of our hearts and what we most need.

God's Attributes

- generous
- kind
- loving
- overruling

SING THE SONG

Reflect on Romans 8:32; 1 Timothy 6:17–19; James 1:16–17; and 2 Peter 1:3–4.

Psalm

~~~ 146 ~~~

Be Still and Know

THEME

As the hope and help of his people, God is worthy of praise.

HARMONY

Psalm 146 was composed by the Sons of Korah to rejoice in the gift of Zion, or Jerusalem, the special city where God revealed his presence, protection, and power to his people. The Sons of Korah were appointed by King David to serve in music ministry at the sanctuary of God's house.

SINGING IN TUNE

In every beginning and every ending, God is worthy of praise, because he governs not only beginnings and endings but also everything in between. The psalmist does that in his song—*hallelujah* is his first word and his last. God alone can care fully for his people, so for them to rely on human beings for what only God can provide is foolish (vv. 3–4). Those who trust in the Lord are blessed, because the help they hope for is sure to come. The One who created the world can work everything in it for the good of his people (vv. 5–6). He alone is always faithful to keep his promises. Only God never grows weary of providing for the poor and needy, and only he can deliver from evil and sin and their blinding effects (vv. 7–9). And those who belong to him will enjoy these blessings for all eternity (v. 10).

MUSICAL NOTES

God's Grace

All the blessings named in this song foreshadow the coming of Christ—our greatest gift. He came to free us from the prison of our sin and open our blind eyes. We know the song was really about him, because he said so: "The Spirit of the Lord is upon me, because he has anointed me to proclaim good news to the poor. He has sent me to proclaim liberty to the captives and recovering of sight to the blind, to set at liberty those who are oppressed, to proclaim the year of the Lord's favor" (Luke 4:18–19), and after that, he said, "Today this Scripture has been fulfilled in your hearing" (Luke 4:21).

God's Attributes

- creating
- delivering
- hope-giving
- providing
- saving
- trustworthy

SING THE SONG

Ponder the link between Psalm 146; Isaiah 61:1–3; and Luke 4:16–21.

Psalm

~~ 147 ~~

Our Great King

THEME

Nothing and no one are outside the sphere of God's sovereignty.

HARMONY

Psalm 147 was composed by the Sons of Korah to praise God as the ultimate King over all the earth. The Sons of Korah were appointed by King David to serve in music ministry. While the song was given to God's people to sing, it invites the whole world to come and worship.

SINGING IN TUNE

God sheds the blessings of his favor most especially on his own people, yet nothing escapes his notice, and he directs the course of everything and everyone. He guides the galaxies, directing each star on its course, just as he knows exactly the right remedy for every broken heart (vv. 1–4). Truly "his understanding is beyond measure" (v. 5). The song reveals a glimpse of God's heart—specific things God delights in. One of those is humility. He loves to lift up those who make themselves low (v. 6). Another is trust. God is delighted when we reject the illusion of self-sufficiency and depend fully on him (vv. 10–11). He is also pleased when we live in hopeful expectation, anticipating displays of his love and kindness in our lives (v. 11). Bracing ourselves for the future with a glass-half-empty outlook isn't wise; it's a self-made shield against the vulnerability that goes hand in hand with hope. In the psalmist's day,

God showed special favor to Jerusalem and his people who lived there, blessing them with strength, peace, and prosperity (vv. 12–14). In so doing, those outside the nation of Israel would long to become insiders, thereby knowing for themselves the One who rules creation (vv. 15–20).

MUSICAL NOTES

God's Grace

"The LORD . . . gathers the outcasts of Israel" (v. 2). By God's grace, through faith in Christ, we have been brought in and made part of God's special people. Adopted into his family, we receive all the blessings he has for his children—protection, provision, and personal knowledge of our Lord. We sing our own hallelujah because "in love he predestined us for adoption to himself as sons through Jesus Christ, according to the purpose of his will, to the praise of his glorious grace, with which he has blessed us in the Beloved" (Eph. 1:4–6).

God's Attributes

- caring
- healing
- praiseworthy
- providing
- saving
- sovereign

SING THE SONG

Explain how Galatians 4:1–7 helps you sing Psalm 147.

Psalm

·❧· 148 ·❦·

Let Heaven and Nature Sing

THEME

God is the Creator of all and the Redeemer of his people.

HARMONY

Psalm 148 is a praise hymn that calls all of creation to showcase God's glory.

SINGING IN TUNE

How amazing that the Holy Spirit, who inspired this psalm, saw fit to work through human beings to call even angels to give praise (v. 2). Sun, moon, and stars are also called upon. This isn't just poetic language. Every aspect of creation glorifies God simply by doing what God designed it to do (vv. 7–10). Every sunset declares that God is praiseworthy, along with the full moon rising and the shooting star arcing across the sky. The same is true down here on earth. Both the explosive power of a hurricane and a warm summer breeze sing God's praise. From frolicking dolphins to hardworking ants, from the yellow trumpet of a daffodil tipped toward heaven to the haunting fragrance of a stargazer lily—God is praised. Human beings, as the pinnacle of God's creation, call everything else to give praise. His very own people are to praise him most of all (vv. 11–13). Not only has he given us life, but he also sustains us in it and preserves us for himself (v. 14).

MUSICAL NOTES

God's Grace

Everything in creation praises God just by being what it is; even so, the fulfillment of this psalm awaits a future day. For the time being, all of creation's songs are mingled with groans because of man's sin (Rom. 8:22). But God has indeed raised up a "horn" (v. 14) for his people—his Son—through whom redemption from sin has come. Because of him a day is coming when creation's praise will no longer be tainted, and for that reason, we sing our praise with hope. "I consider that the sufferings of this present time are not worth comparing with the glory that is to be revealed to us. . . . For the creation was subjected to futility, not willingly, but because of him who subjected it in hope that the creation itself will be set free from its bondage to corruption and obtain the freedom of the glory of the children of God" (Rom. 8:18–21).

God's Attributes

- creating
- redeeming
- sustaining

SING THE SONG

Consider how Colossians 1:15–20 helps you offer praise to God through Psalm 148.

Psalm

✣ 149 ✣

Sing a New Song

THEME

God works his will and ways in and through the lives of his people.

HARMONY

Psalm 149 is another praise hymn composed for singing in public worship.

SINGING IN TUNE

New songs rise up from all who know their God because the supply of his blessings never runs dry. In this song God is praised for establishing a reciprocal relationship with his people. He makes them glad, and in turn he takes pleasure in them; they walk with him in humble submission, and he adorns them with all the blessings of salvation (vv. 1–4). There is yet another reason to sing a new song—God will work through his people to banish evil (vv. 6–9). One day those who refuse to submit will be judged, and God has determined to carry out this judgment through those who belong to him. Singing about judgment might seem harsh, but that's only because we don't yet love God or hate evil as we one day will. When we have been fully transformed into the likeness of Christ—a work already underway in those united to him by faith—our orientation will be so utterly fixed on God that we will fully rejoice in the destruction of evil and its every manifestation. Even now, however, we can rejoice that God has planned such an honor for us.

MUSICAL NOTES

God's Grace

God adorns the humble with salvation, but the proud and unrepentant—those who reject him—will sooner or later be condemned. In both ways God is glorified because in both he demonstrates that he is true to his character. We who are under his mercy can rejoice in our salvation, while we also warn the lost of what awaits them if they refuse to repent. Before the day comes when the two-edged sword is placed in our hands, we can take up the sword of the Spirit, the Word of God (Eph. 6:17), and call the lost to trust in Jesus as their Savior and Lord.

God's Attributes

- just
- relational
- saving

SING THE SONG

Consider how 1 Timothy 2:1–6 provides application for Psalm 149.

Psalm

~ 150 ~

Praise the Lord!

THEME

Those who know their God sing with pure praise.

HARMONY

This final song in the Psalter is, fittingly, a praise hymn. Psalm 150 begins and ends decisively with the word *hallelujah*, a call to praise the Lord.

SINGING IN TUNE

As God's people assemble, an exuberant call to worship is issued (v. 1). With a variety of instruments and even dance, he is praised both for who he is and for what he does, and the entire creation is called to join in (vv. 2–6). Here we find no sorrow, fear, or pending calamity from which rescue is needed. No doubt those singing the song had problems of various kinds, but there are times when the greatest trust is demonstrated by an absence of petition. Setting aside personal cares to focus exclusively on the Lord is itself a form of praise, a way of acknowledging God's all-knowing, sovereign care for us and that we believe the words of Jesus: "Your Father knows what you need before you ask him" (Matt. 6:8). Pure praise is a fit ending to the song book of Scripture.

MUSICAL NOTES

God's Grace

The joyful, God-focused manner in which the Psalter ends foreshadows another ending. One day, every song we sing will be nothing but praise.

All God's people, those united to him by faith in Jesus, will sing together in the new heavens and the new earth. There, "they will be his people, and God himself will be with them as their God. He will wipe away every tear from their eyes, and death shall be no more, neither shall there be mourning, nor crying, nor pain anymore, for the former things have passed away" (Rev. 21:3–4).

God's Attributes

- praiseworthy

SING THE SONG

Consider what Ephesians 5:18–20 and Colossians 3:15–17 add to your understanding of Psalm 150.

Appendix 1

Preparing a Group
Study of Psalms

Creating a Bible study in Psalms may seem daunting, but by keeping in mind a few principles and following a few steps, you'll see how doable it actually is. The notes provided here will help you to both prepare and participate in a group study.

PRIORITIZE THE POETRY

First things first: *the poetry is important.* In fact, each of the 150 psalms is a poem—originally meant to be sung—and each one is made up of verses written in a form called *parallelism.* There are two primary reasons that this matters so much. First, the authors of the psalms used a poetic structure in order to convey a certain message. Second, poetry takes literary license that regular prose does not, making use of symbols and images in creative ways. Therefore, because we can identify the psalms as poetry, we are able to avoid interpreting something literally that was meant to be understood figuratively. So when the psalmist complains, "My tears have been my food day and night" (Ps. 42:3), the poetical structure guides our interpretation: he is describing the extent of his pain, not an actual meal of tears. Finally, when we think of poetry, what usually comes to mind are words and lines carefully crafted to rhyme. The poetry style of ancient Israel does rhyme, but unlike the rhyming sounds we're familiar with, the poetry of the psalms has rhyming *thoughts.*[6] Look, for example, at the first verse of Psalm 19:

The heavens declare the glory of God,

and the sky above proclaims his handiwork.

Can you see how the second line echoes the first? The second line is simply meant to intensify the first line. That's how the poetry of Psalms is structured. See appendix 3 for the different types of parallelism to watch for as you study the psalms.

So, now, tuck away in your mind the importance of the poetry as we move ahead in our study preparation.

PREPARE THE STUDY

Identify

We want to begin with a big-picture view of the psalm to be studied. We do that by asking questions in order to identify particular characteristics about it. Here, *context* is key. Our overarching goal is to understand what God has revealed. Too often we begin with ourselves—what *we* get out of the psalm rather than what *God* has put into it. In order to rightly relate to our heavenly Father, we have to orient our thinking upward rather than inward, and this begins with examining the original context of the psalm. So we ask questions (and this is precisely where the material in *Sing a New Song* can prove most useful):

1. *Who wrote it?* Many psalms don't identify the author, but we can get started on understanding the original setting if an author's name is supplied.

2. *Is a particular occasion or event indicated?* Often we are given a general idea of whether a psalm was written to thank God for blessings or to plead for God's help in troublesome times. Other psalms name a specific occasion for which the psalm was composed. In such cases, many Bibles supply cross-references that direct you to the places in Scripture where you can read about that occasion in greater detail.

3. *How is the psalm best classified?* The Psalter contains psalms of lament, of praise, and of contrition for sin, as well as those

celebrating the king of Israel and the holy city Jerusalem. Classifying the psalm is helpful in grasping the original context. For a list of the various psalm types, see appendix 3.

4. *How would you summarize the theme of the psalm?*

5. *What attributes of God are readily seen?*

6. *What emotions are indicated by the psalmist's words?* This isn't a touchy-feely sort of issue; it's a vital aspect of what the psalms are intended to communicate. God created us as emotional beings, and he invites us to come into his presence in all our varied moods. Doing so reverently is an indicator of spiritual health and honest, robust faith.

7. *What particular figures of speech does the psalmist employ?* The psalms contain metaphors, hyperbole, paradoxes, similes, and symbols—all as a means of communicating something particular. Identifying speech features helps us understand what the psalmist is getting at and guards us against possibly misapplying the psalm to our own time and circumstances. See appendix 3 for a list of the various speech figures found in the psalms.

Now that we've asked questions and identified the context of the psalm, we can go in for a closer look and shape material for personal reflection or group discussion.

SHAPE YOUR STUDY

The way to get to the heart of a psalm in order to apply it personally is to continue asking questions. At this point, after we've identified the big picture, we focus in on the specific content. We'll illustrate with Psalm 3.

Sample Study: Psalm 3

As we proceed, we keep in mind our Psalm 3 big picture: the psalm is a lament written by David when his son Absalom sought to kill him, as the superscription at the beginning tells us. We see that David is greatly distressed, but he trusts that God is a powerful defender. We can identify

331

synthetic parallelism in verse 1, because the second line repeats the idea of the first line. From that we know the psalmist is emphasizing something important, in this case, the great depth of David's distress. We also find a *metaphor* in verse 3, where God is likened to a shield. Here we see the importance of being able to recognize figures of speech—we don't want to misunderstand God as a literal shield. Rather, we are meant to know him as *like* a shield—strong and protecting. While we're on the big-picture subject, let me caution against getting bogged down in technicality. In other words, don't stress about identifying poetry type and figures of speech in every verse. Simply be aware of them and note them as they jump out at you.

With that in mind, we move inward, shaping questions to ponder or discuss with a group.

3:1	What is happening, and to whom? Use the superscription at the beginning to aid you here. Your Bible will likely direct you to 2 Samuel 15:14-17.
3:2	What does this verse reveal about the enemies' tactics? What does this teach us? Where else in Scripture is this type of trouble exposed?
3:3	In what way does David's thinking shift focus here? How is his shift indicated? What three things are noted about God in verse 3, and what does each one mean?
3:4	Given the strength of both the enemy and God, what does David do, and how does he do it? What does this teach us about prayer? How does God respond? What is meant by God's "holy hill"?
3:5	How has praying helped David? What does this verse teach us about sleep as a spiritual issue?
3:6	Describe David's confidence. What has brought it to the surface?
3:7	What does David ask God to do? How does an understanding of parallelism help us get the meaning of David's prayer request in line 1? Why is David confident that God will answer his prayer? What do lines 3-4 reveal about God's character?
3:8	How has David's mood changed from the beginning of the psalm? What does his closing reveal about God and about salvation? What does David pray for in the last line? What does this reveal about God's blessings?

So this is how we do it. You can adapt this format to any psalm, beginning with the big picture and then working inward to ask questions of each verse or stanza. Your next task is to identify which psalms to study.

CHOOSING PSALMS FOR YOUR STUDY

You have total freedom in choosing which psalms to study, since each psalm is a self-contained unit. In other words, you needn't be concerned about somehow clustering them incorrectly. So one factor might be the number of weeks you plan to meet. Another consideration is the depth of understanding your group has about God and what it means to walk with him. New believers might benefit from psalms that emphasize trust. Longtime Christians might want to delve into the psalms that contain some challenging theological truths, such as God's judgment on sin, or psalms that reveal God's overarching work of salvation through history. Or do some of each! Appendix 3 offers one way to classify the psalms, if you'd like some guidance getting started.

Appendix 2

Getting Real and Drawing Near

Studying the Psalms Devotionally

In our feelings-oriented culture, where emotions are allowed to dictate, well, just about everything, it can be a challenge to figure out how emotions factor in to Christian discipleship. We want to be careful that our authority is God's Word, not our feelings, yet we don't want caution to become suspicion, leaching any credibility out of what we feel. The psalms are incredibly helpful in this regard. From the Psalter we learn that emotions are meant to be an instrument of discipleship rather than a hindrance to it. The psalms

> express a wide variety of emotions, including: love and adoration toward God, sorrow over sin, dependence on God in desperate circumstances, the battle of fear and trust, walking with God even when the way seems dark, thankfulness for God's care, devotion to the word of God, and confidence in the eventual triumph of God's purposes for the world.[7]

No other book of the Bible expresses the range of human feeling so freely.

In light of that, Psalms is a terrific biblical book in which to immerse yourself as a means of exposing your heart more fully to the transforming work of the Holy Spirit and learning how to draw near to God with openness and honesty. Every single psalm expresses at least one emotion, and when set alongside the attributes of God, we have an immense opportunity to deepen both our understanding and enjoyment of the

relationship we have with him through our union with Christ. The en-
tries in *Sing a New Song* can help you engage in this sort of devotional
study. I'll illustrate again with Psalm 3.

AN APPROACH FOR GETTING REAL AND DRAWING NEAR
Prepare

As you might recall, Psalm 3 is a lament written by David when his son
Absalom sought to kill him. We see in the psalm that David is greatly
distressed, but he trusts that God is a powerful defender. As we ponder
his song, we can identify a range of emotions:

- distress
- anguish
- helplessness
- fear
- confidence
- trust
- peace

These emotions are evidenced from David's words, from the tone of
those words, and from the circumstances he writes about. So, for example, we can rightly add *anguish* to our emotions list, even though it isn't
explicitly stated, when we realize that his enemy here, the one seeking
to kill him, was his very own son.

Alongside our list of emotions we add the revealed attributes of God:

	Emotions	God's Attributes
	distress	
	anguish	protecting
	helplessness	listening
	fear	sustaining
	trust	saving
	peace	
	confidence	

Notice how David's emotions change as the psalm progresses, as he focuses on God and God's character. Which of God's attributes connect to which of David's emotions, and how do David's feelings change in the process? For each psalm you study, create a chart of your own and draw lines to note correspondences. Or you can simply write them out:

- Helplessness becomes confidence because God hears his cries.
- Distress becomes peace because God is his protector.
- Fear becomes trust because God has promised to save him.
- Anguish becomes peace because God sustains him.

There is no right or wrong here in terms of making connections. All David's emotions are influenced as he ponders each of God's attributes and prays. Writing out correspondences you see is a simple way to make the transformation more concrete.

Personalize

Now make it personal. Are you experiencing any (or all) of the emotions we've identified in Psalm 3? If so, what in your life has triggered these feelings? Can you identify additional emotions or variations on the ones in this list? After you've identified how you are feeling, spend a few minutes pondering the attributes of God found in the psalm and then connect them, as David did, to your present circumstances. How can the facts of God's protection, listening ear, sustaining grace, and promise to save impact your current thoughts and feelings?

Pray

The final step is prayer. Pray Psalm 3, or portions of it, and then make it personal:

- Lord, I feel utterly helpless in this situation, but I believe you have heard my cries for deliverance and that you'll save me out of this somehow, some way.

- Father, I can't seem to overcome my fear, so I ask to know your protective care in a way that deepens my trust in you.

- Dear God, I dread going to bed because anxiety has been keeping me awake, but I am reminded that you're the One who sustains my life, so I pray for help to be mindful of that as I prepare for bed tonight.

THE WHOLE RANGE

If you decide to embark on a personal study like this one, don't limit yourself to just one kind of psalm. Be sure to include psalms of praise and thanksgiving as well as lament. Our relationship with God in Christ is intimate, and like all such relationships, intimacy develops as we share both the highs and the lows—every aspect of shared life.

Appendix 3

Types and Categories

PSALM TYPES

If you do some research, you'll quickly discover that scholars use different ways to classify psalms. Keep in mind that these are man-made categories; in other words, hold them loosely. Use them merely as a study tool. And also keep in mind that some psalms fall into more than one category, and other psalms don't seem to fit well into any of those we use here.

Confidence psalms. These psalms express confidence in God's care, even when (perhaps especially when) danger threatens.

Historical psalms. Such psalms reflect on God's work in the world throughout history, most especially in his dealings with his own people.

Imprecatory psalms. Sometimes the hardest to study and understand, these psalms contain prayers requesting God to deliver judgment and destruction on evil people. We can make sense of this type of psalm by taking into account the teaching of God's Word as a whole. As we do, we realize that these prayers for destruction weren't motivated by revenge but by a desire for the triumph of righteousness over evil.

Laments. The majority of psalms fall into this category. The laments express painful emotions that arise from perplexity, anguish, and at times discouragement. Some psalms contain the lament of an individual; others express community-wide trouble. In either case, a note of hope is usually present, as well as words of confidence in God.

Messianic psalms. A subset of royal psalms, these most clearly fore-shadow the coming King, the Messiah, Jesus Christ.

Penitential psalms. Psalms that include an acknowledgment of sin—whether individual or corporate—are often placed in this category.

Pilgrimage psalms. God's people sang these journeying psalms when they traveled to Jerusalem to worship God. Travelers sang together to stir up joyful anticipation of entering God's presence. The Psalms of Ascent (120–134) fall into this category.

Praise psalms. Many psalms are songs celebrating God's greatness and the privileges that come to his people.

Royal psalms. Some of the psalms rejoice over the gift of a God-appointed king, men from the line of David, because such kings were to serve as ambassadors of God's protection and provision for his people. Ultimately, these psalms point forward to Jesus, the King of kings. In keeping are psalms that celebrate Zion (Jerusalem) because it was the place God appointed for his people to gather and worship him and live together under his protection.

Thanksgiving psalms. These psalms express gratitude for answered prayer or, at times, anticipation of an answer. Both individuals and the gathered community of God's people offered thanksgiving psalms.

Wisdom psalms. Themes and language borrowed from the Bible's Wisdom Literature are threaded into these psalms. In that regard, you'll often be able to detect similarities to Job, Proverbs, Ecclesiastes, and Song of Solomon.

POETRY PARALLELISM

Again you will find that scholars differ in how they classify the poetry in psalms. I've included a sampling of some of the primary categories here. The primary thing to keep in mind is that the poetic lines are used purposefully, for emphasis.

Synonymous parallelism. The second line says the same thing as the first line.

> You sit and speak against your brother;
>> you slander your own mother's son. (Ps. 50:20)

Antithetic parallelism. The second line stands in contrast to the first line. Hint: Look for the word *but*.

> For the LORD knows the way of the righteous,
>> but the way of the wicked will perish. (Ps. 1:6)

Emblematic parallelism. The second line offers a comparison to the first line. Watch for a simile or a metaphor.

> He is like a lion eager to tear,
>> as a young lion lurking in ambush. (Ps. 17:12)

LITERARY TERMS

Keep an eye out for particular literary devices. The psalm writers used these purposefully to convey powerful emotions and ideas.

Metaphor. A comparison that doesn't use the words *like* or *as*:

> "The LORD is my rock." (Ps. 18:2)

Simile. A comparison or figure of speech that contains *like* or *as*:

> Your righteousness is like the mountains of God;
>> your judgments are like the great deep;
>> man and beast you save, O LORD. (Ps. 36:6)

Personification. Human attributes are applied to an object, an animal, or a particular quality:

> Lift up your heads, O gates!
>> And be lifted up, O ancient doors,
>> that the King of glory may come in. (Ps. 24:7)

Hyperbole. Exaggeration is used deliberately to intensify a point:

> You brought us into the net;
>> you laid a crushing burden on our backs. (Ps. 66:11)

Apostrophe. The author speaks to someone or something not actually present:

> Praise him, sun and moon,
>> praise him, all you shining stars! (Psalm 148:3)

For Further Study

DEVOTIONALS

Keller, Timothy, and Kathy Keller. *The Songs of Jesus: A Year of Daily Devotions in the Psalms*. New York: Viking, 2015.

Drawing on their personal study and reflection, Tim and Kathy Keller assembled this daily devotional to share all they have learned through their focus on Psalms.

Motyer, Alec. *Psalms by the Day*. Ross-shire, UK: Christian Focus, 2016.

Alec Motyer leads us through Psalms in this devotional guide. He explains each psalm and then provides thoughts for reflection.

Ortlund, Dane. *ESV Devotional Psalter*. Wheaton, IL: Crossway, 2017.

Any devotional writing by Dane Ortlund is worth adding to your library. Here, each of the 150 psalms is paired with Dane's devotional content, guiding us to interact with and pray through God's Word.

Whitney, Donald S. *Praying the Bible*. Wheaton, IL: Crossway, 2015.

Donald Whitney shows us how to pray through portions of Scripture one line at a time. His book isn't a devotional, but I've placed it under the "Devotionals" subhead because his "Psalms of the Day" chart in the appendixes provides an organized, daily plan for praying through the entire Psalter.

COMMENTARIES

Boice, James Montgomery. *Psalms*. 3 vols. Grand Rapids, MI: Baker, 1994.

This three-volume set comes directly from Dr. Boice's sermon series on Psalms and blends faithful Bible teaching with a pastoral tone.

Kidner, Derek. *Psalms 1–72* and *Psalms 73–150*, Kidner Classic Commentaries. First printed in 1973; repr. Downers Grove, IL: IVP Academic, 2014. Derek Kidner is a well-regarded expert on Psalms (and Proverbs too), so if you are building a study library, this is a good resource to include.

VanGemeren, Willem A. "Psalms." In *The Expositor's Bible Commentary, Volume 5: Psalms, Proverbs, Ecclesiastes, Song of Songs.* Edited by Frank Gaebelein. Grand Rapids, MI: Zondervan, 1991.
I haven't read this one, but it comes highly recommended by theologians I trust.

BIBLE STUDIES

Guthrie, Nancy. *The Wisdom of God: Seeing Jesus in the Psalms and Wisdom Books.* Wheaton, IL: Crossway, 2012.
This ten-week Bible study helps us see where the psalms fit in the context of God's overarching plan of redemption.

Nielson, Kathleen Buswell. *Psalms, Volume 1: Songs Along the Way* and *Psalms, Volume 2: Finding the Way to Prayer and Praise.* Phillipsburg, NJ: P&R, 2009 and 2013.
Kathleen is passionate about careful Bible study and equipping others to study with care.

Notes

1. Many psalm titles include the composer, with wording such as "A Psalm of David." In the original language, the preposition translated "of" could just as easily be translated "belonging to," "authored by," or "about" ("Introduction to the Psalms," in *ESV Study Bible*, ed. Wayne Grudem [Wheaton, IL: Crossway, 2008], 935). *Sing a New Song* assumes the translation "authored by" throughout.
2. *ESV Gospel Transformation Bible*, ed. Bryan Chapell (Wheaton, IL: Crossway, 2013), note on Psalm 35.
3. *ESV Gospel Transformation Bible*, note on Psalm 60.
4. *ESV Study Bible*, note on Psalm 81:1–3.
5. If you find yourself in this state, you might want to read more about divine desertion from one of the Puritans. A place to start is Joel R. Beeke, "Puritans Living in Relationship to Affliction, Desertion, and Sin," *Reformation and Revival* 5, no. 2 (Spring 1996): 100–16, accessed December 8, 2016, https://biblicalstudies.org.uk /pdf/ref-rev/05-2/5-2_beeke2.pdf.
6. A helpful guide for understanding Psalms as poetry is Mark A. Copeland, "The Book of Psalms: A Study Guide with Introductory Comments, Summaries, and Review Questions," accessed April 24, 2017, http://executableoutlines.com/pdf /psa_sg.pdf.
7. "Introduction to the Psalms," in *ESV Study Bible*, 935.

Also Available from
Lydia Brownback

 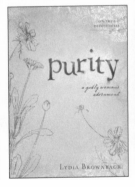 

For more information, visit crossway.org.